Scribble Scrabble Coloring Book For Kids

By Beatrice M. Young

Illustrations by Gayle Crittendon

Scribble Scrabble Coloring Book for Kids

By Beatrice M. Young
Illustrator: Gayle Crittendon

ISBN: 978-0-9863549-3-9

Other Scribble Scrabble Journals:

Scribble Scrabble Writing Journal for Kids
Scribble Scrabble Writing Journal for Kids Book 2
Scribble Scrabble Writing Journal for Kids: A Book of What Ifs

Scribble Scrabble Writing Journals are available at
E'toshaPublications.com, Amazon, Barnes & Noble,
and other online retailers.

Published in 2017 by E'tosha Publications
Printed in the USA by Createspace

Scribble Scrabble Writing Journal for Kids books are available at special
discounts when purchased in quantity for premiums and promotions as
well as fundraising or educational use. For details, contact
beatrice@etoshapublications.com or call 336-280-8321

www.etoshapublications.com

This book is dedicated to God for giving me the gift to write,
To my mother, Rita M. Clay for inspiring me to write,
To the love of my life, Simba and my precious jewels, Ebony, Tasha,
Harmonie, Per'Shawn and Kent for believing in me as a writer,
And to my family and friends for their encouragement and faith in me.

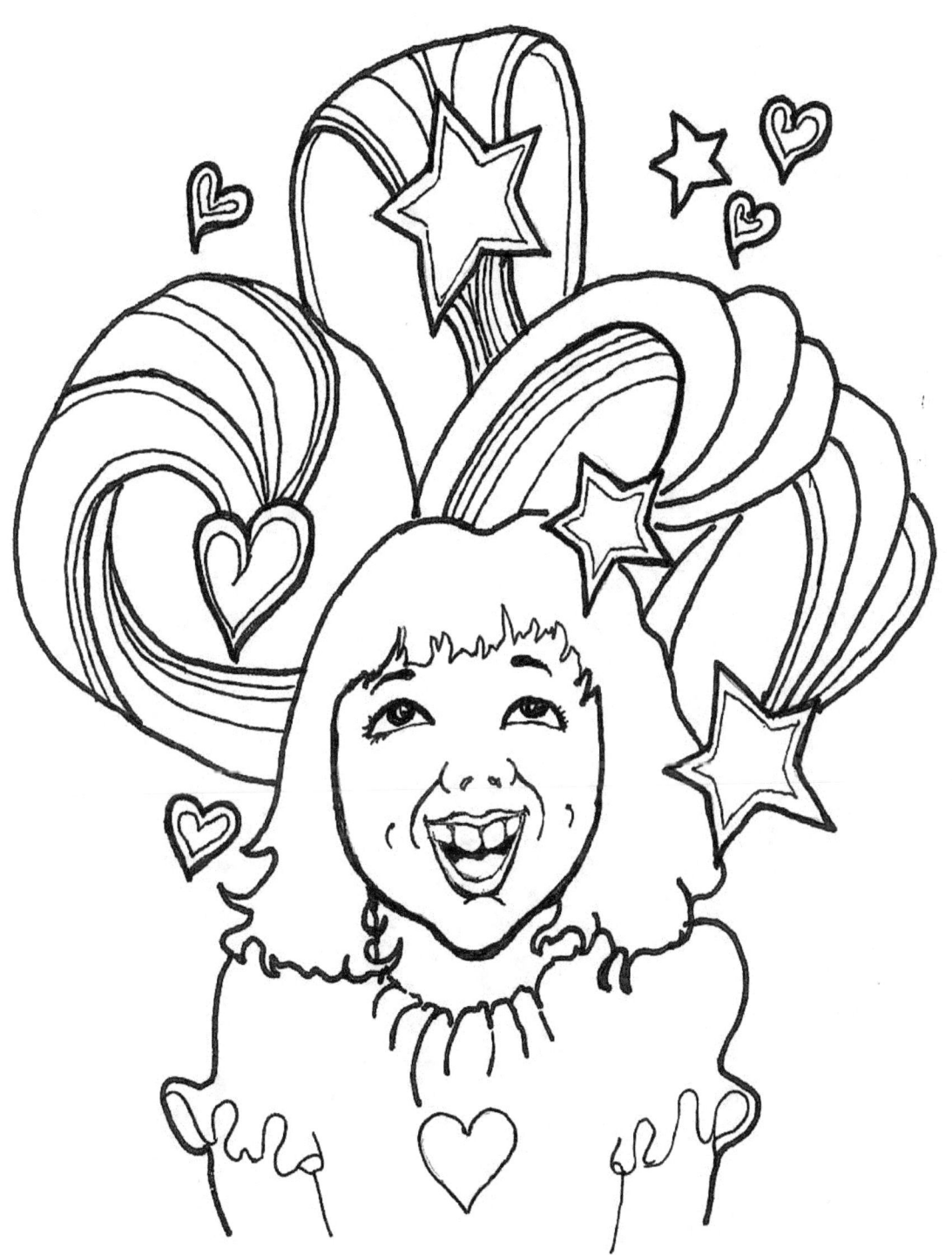

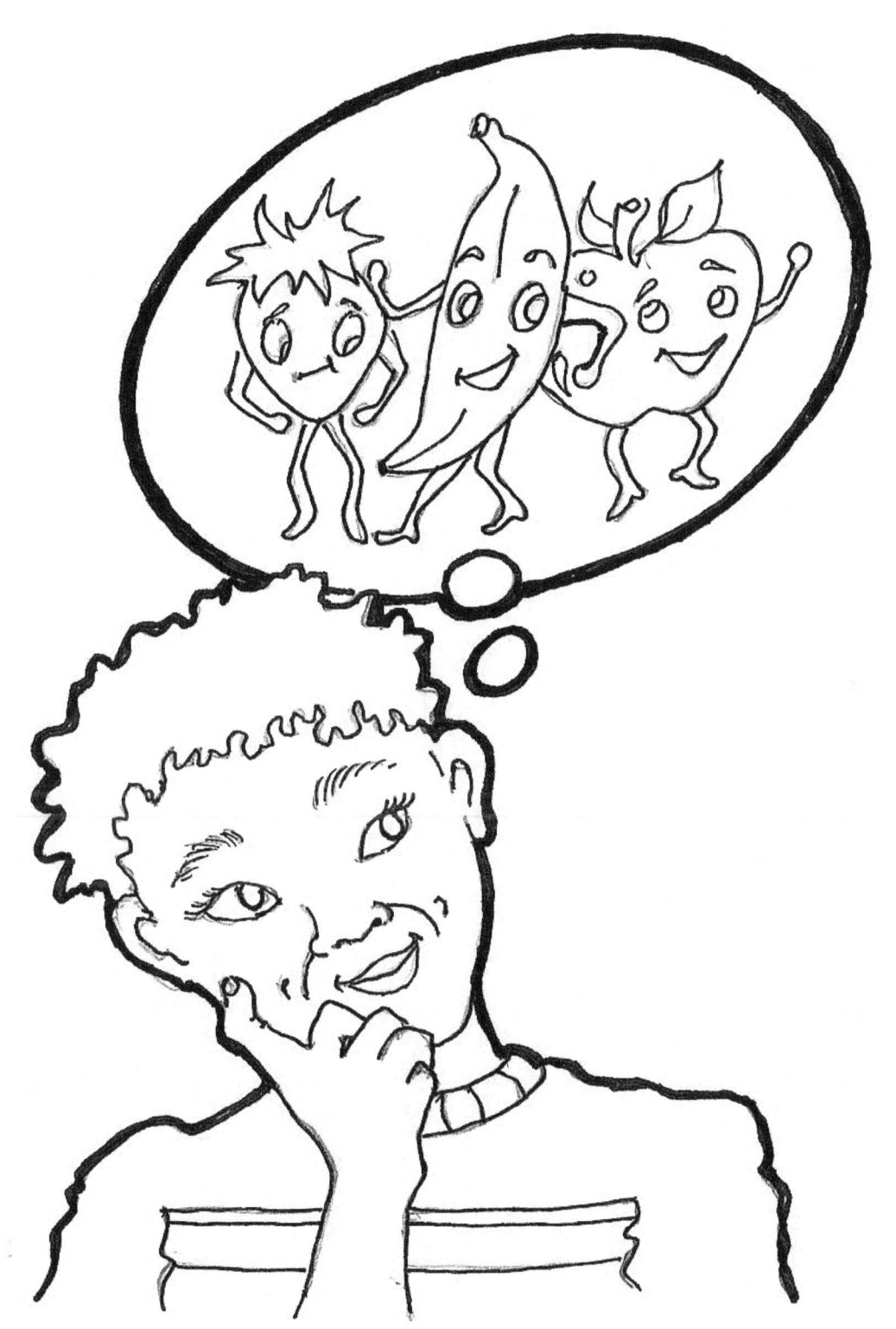

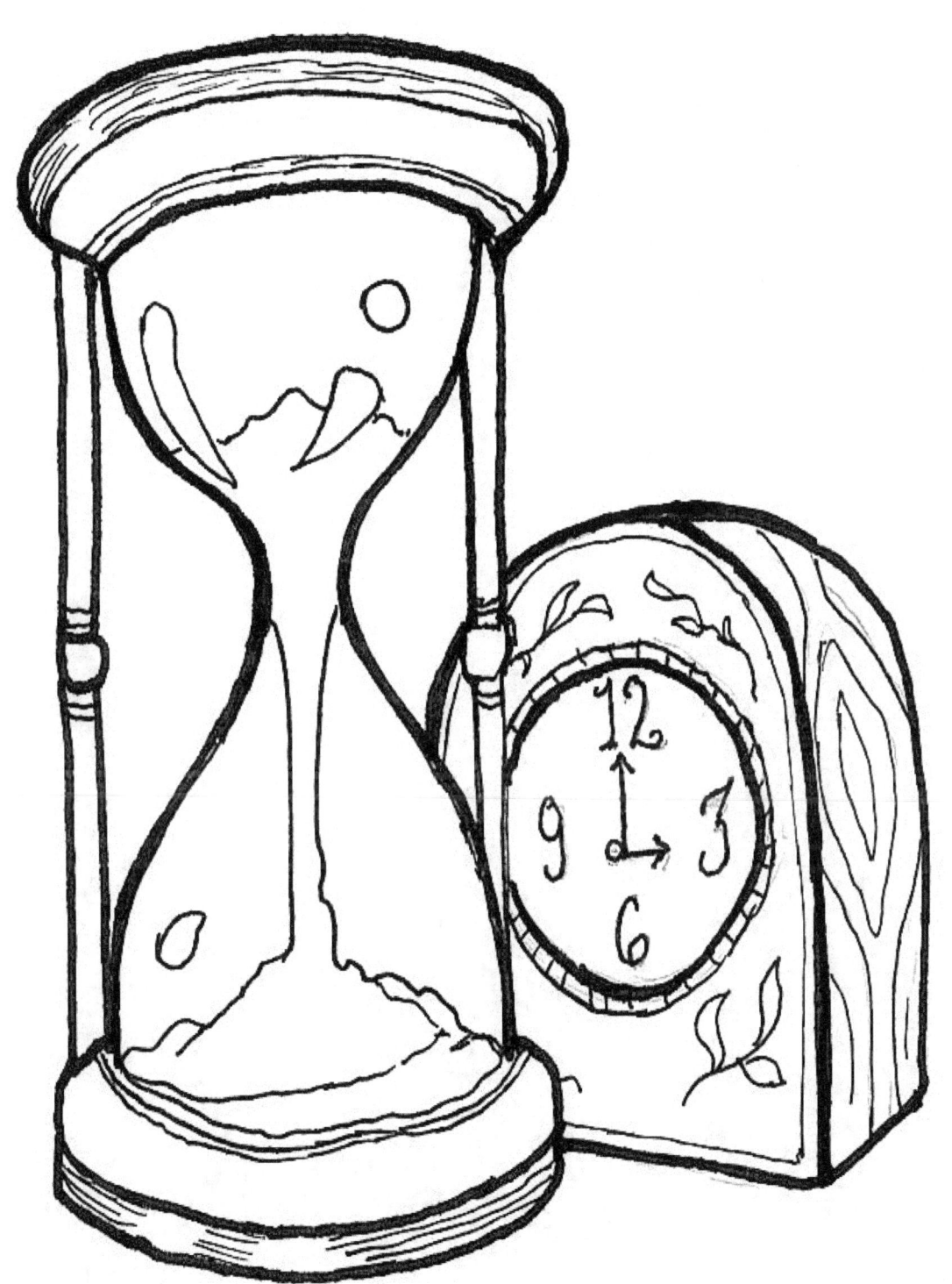

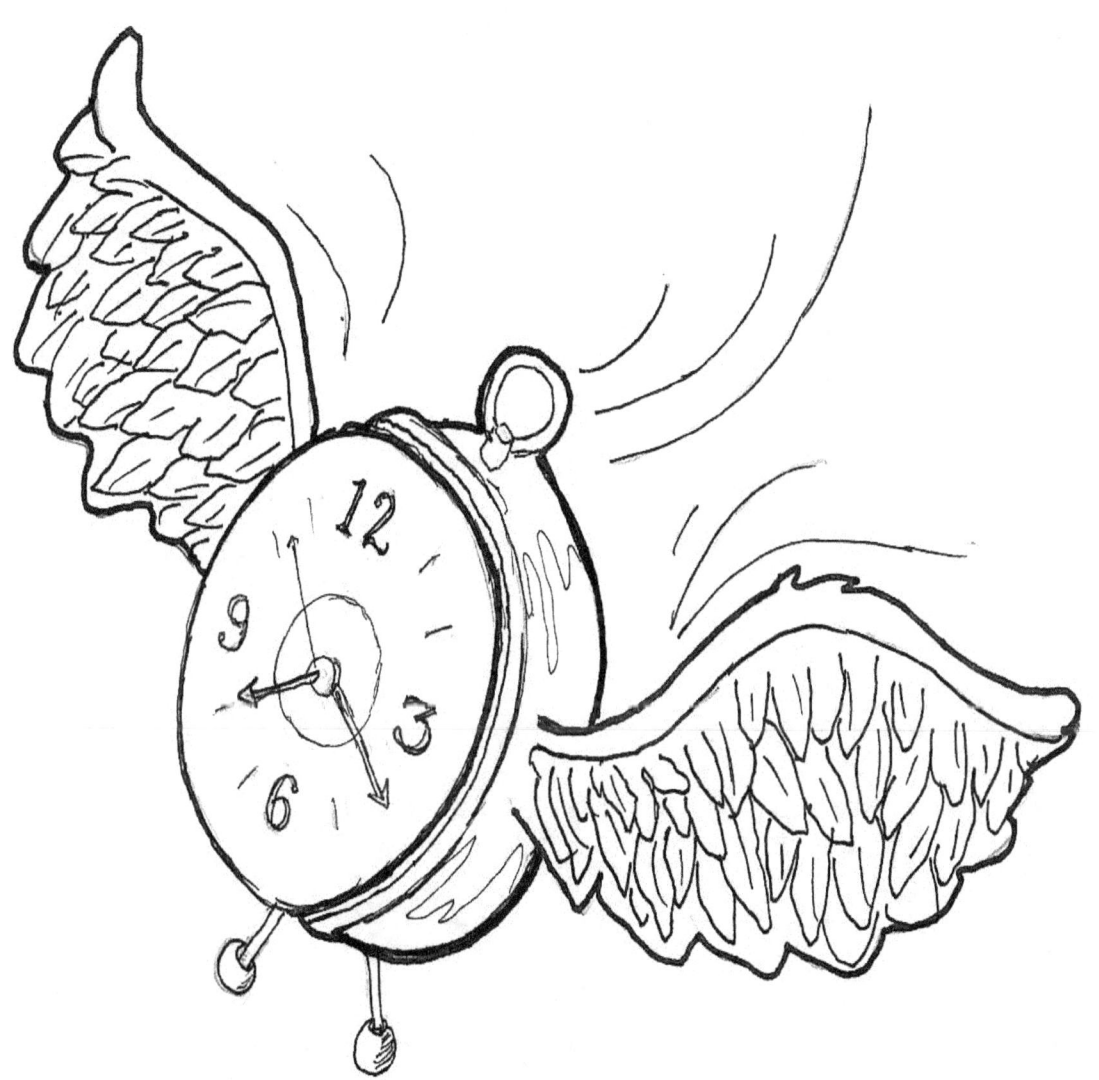

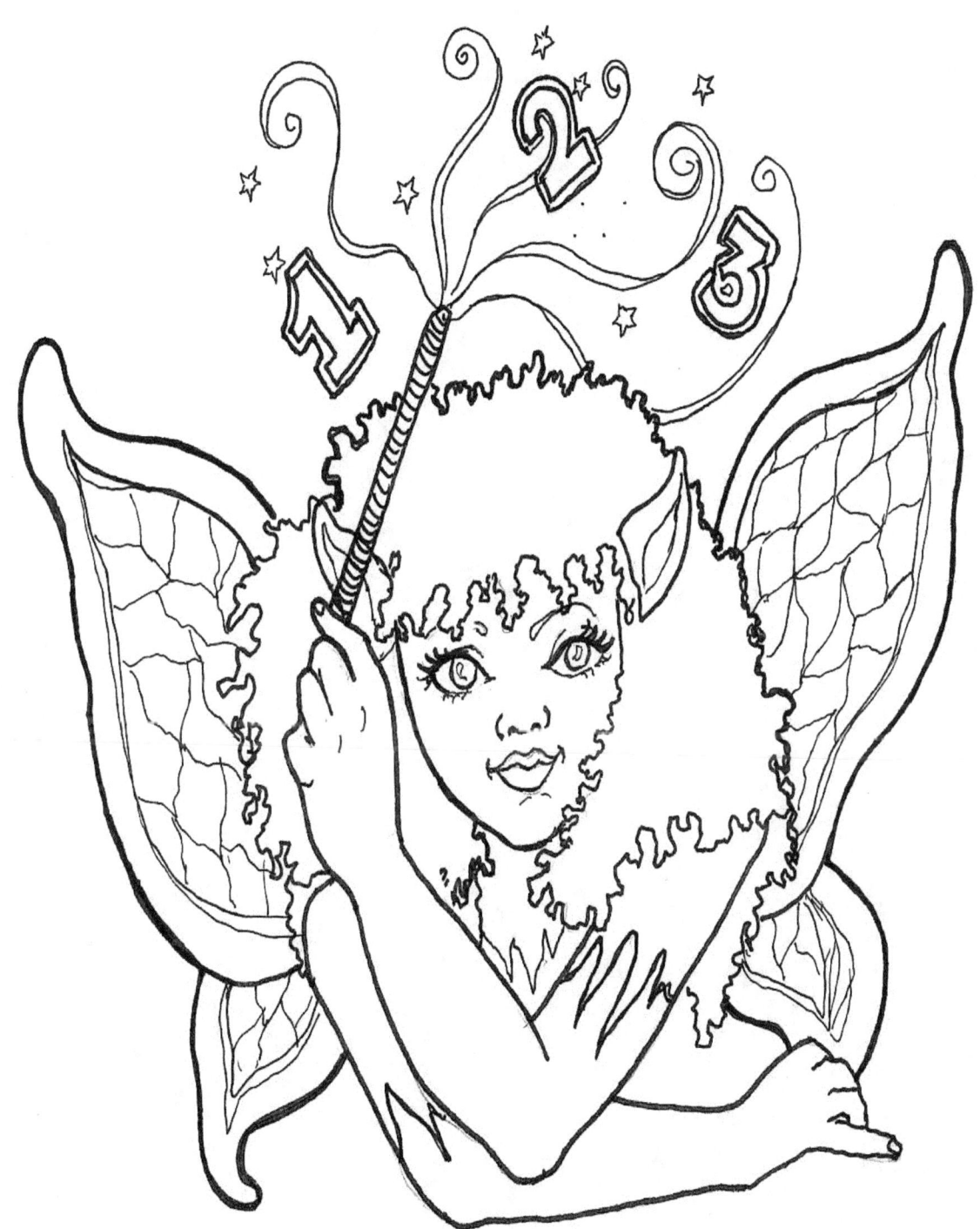

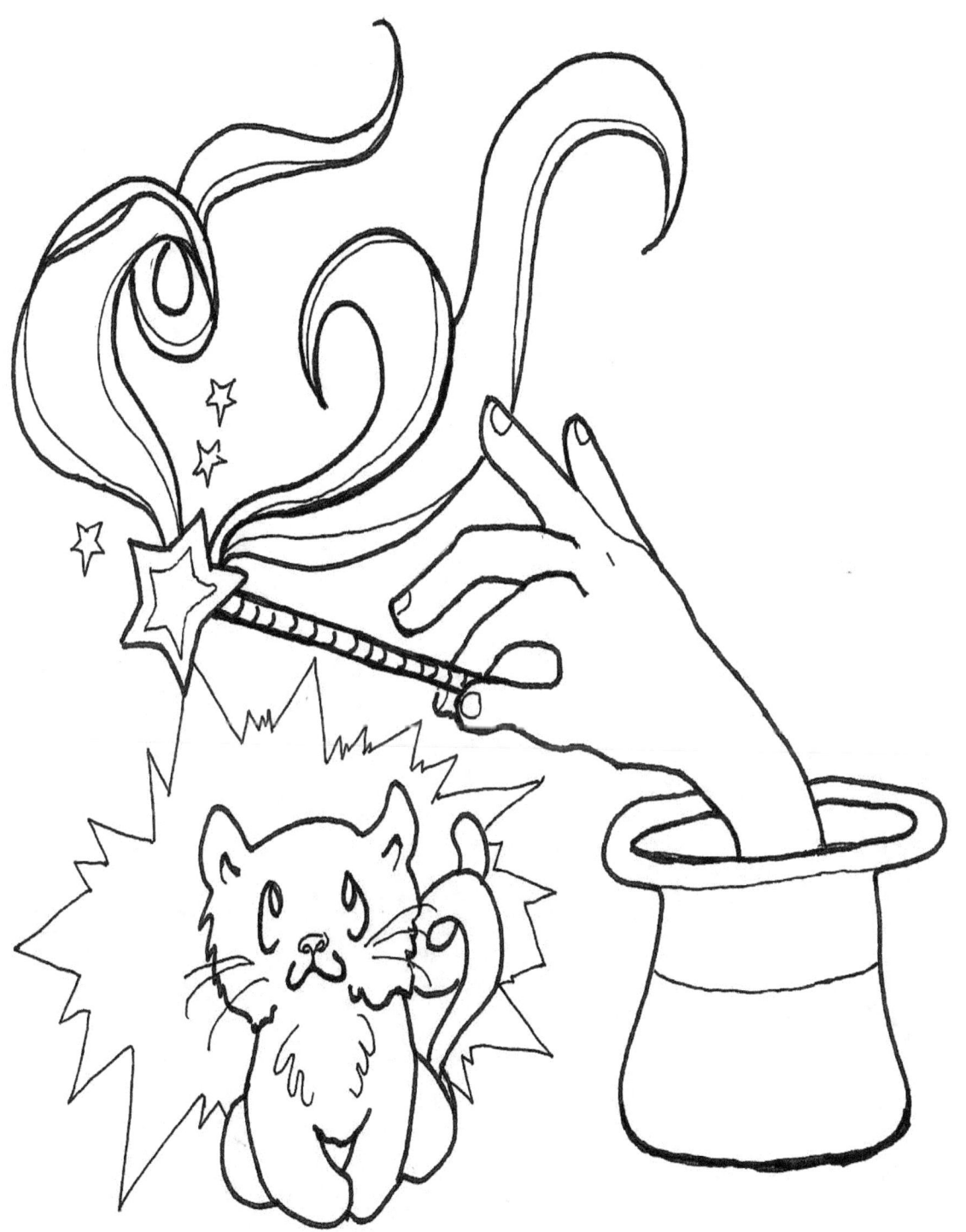

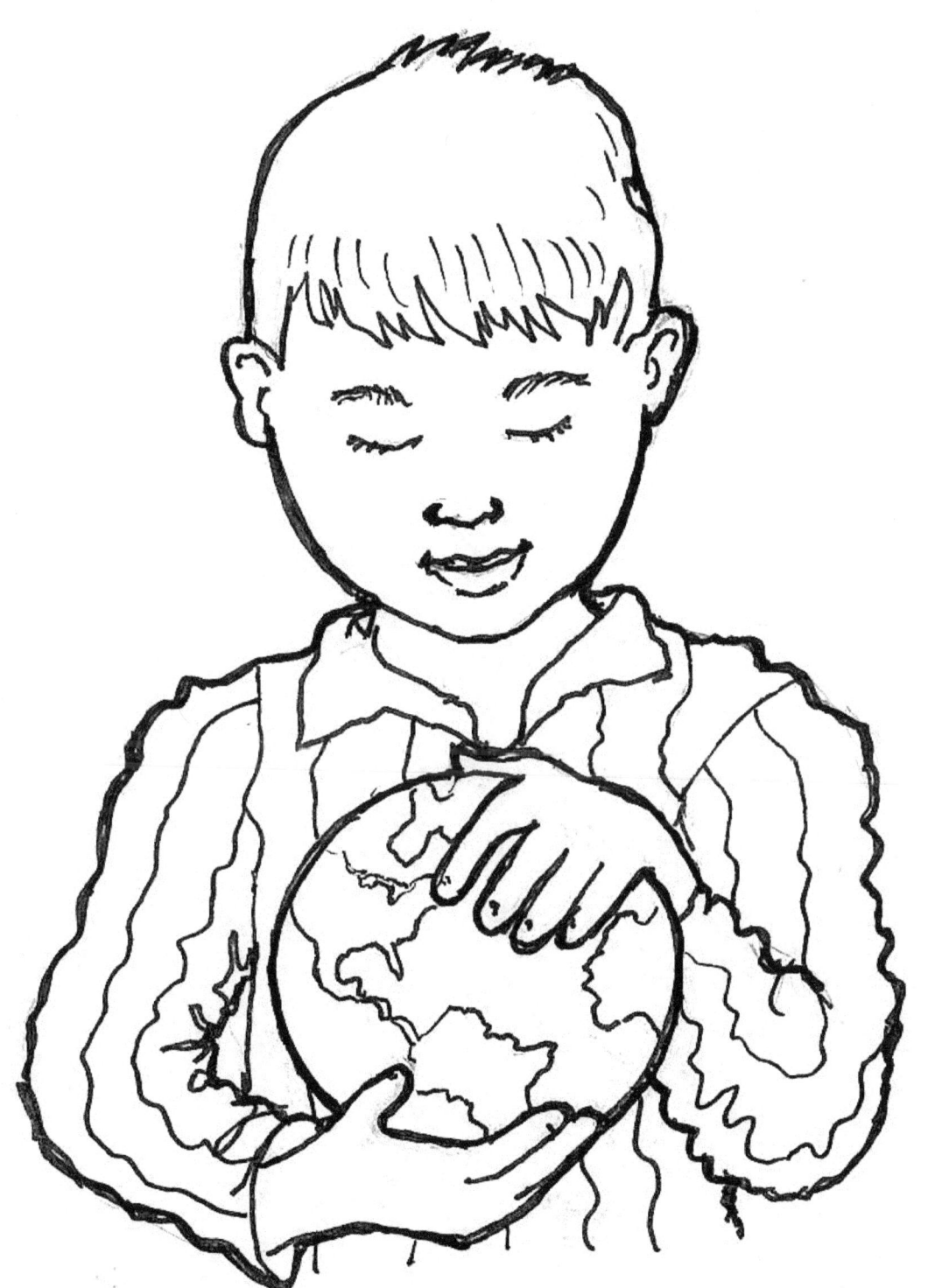

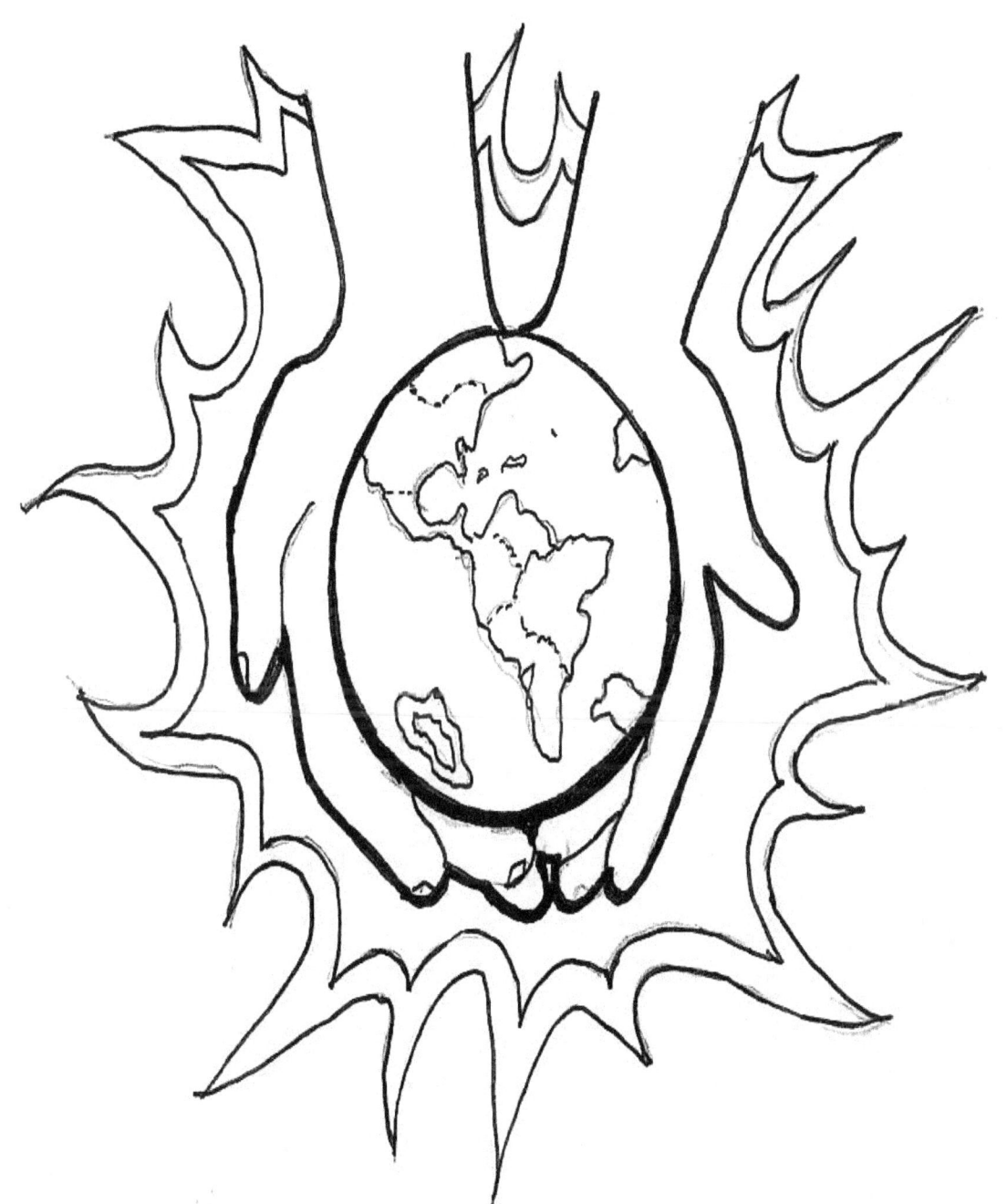

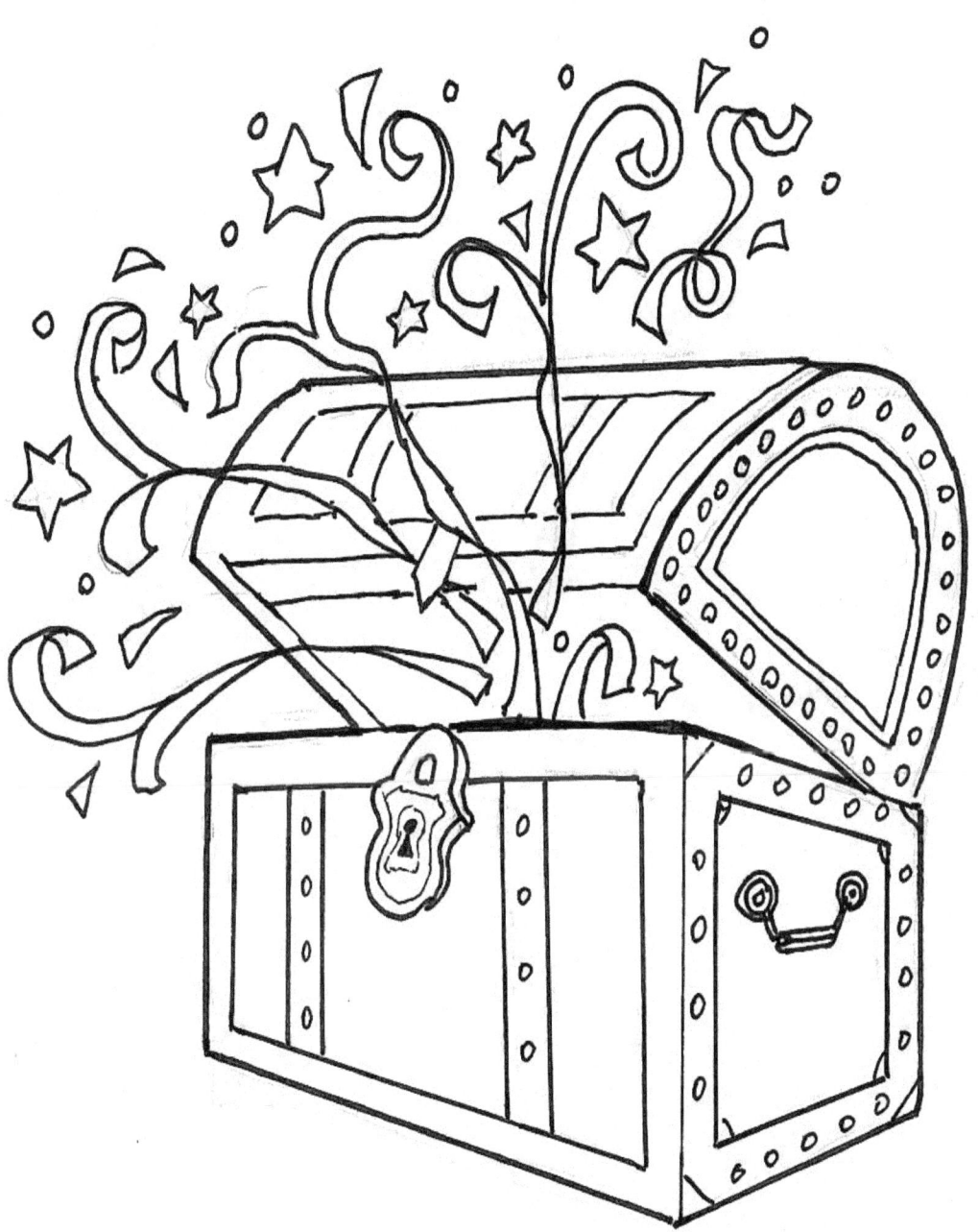

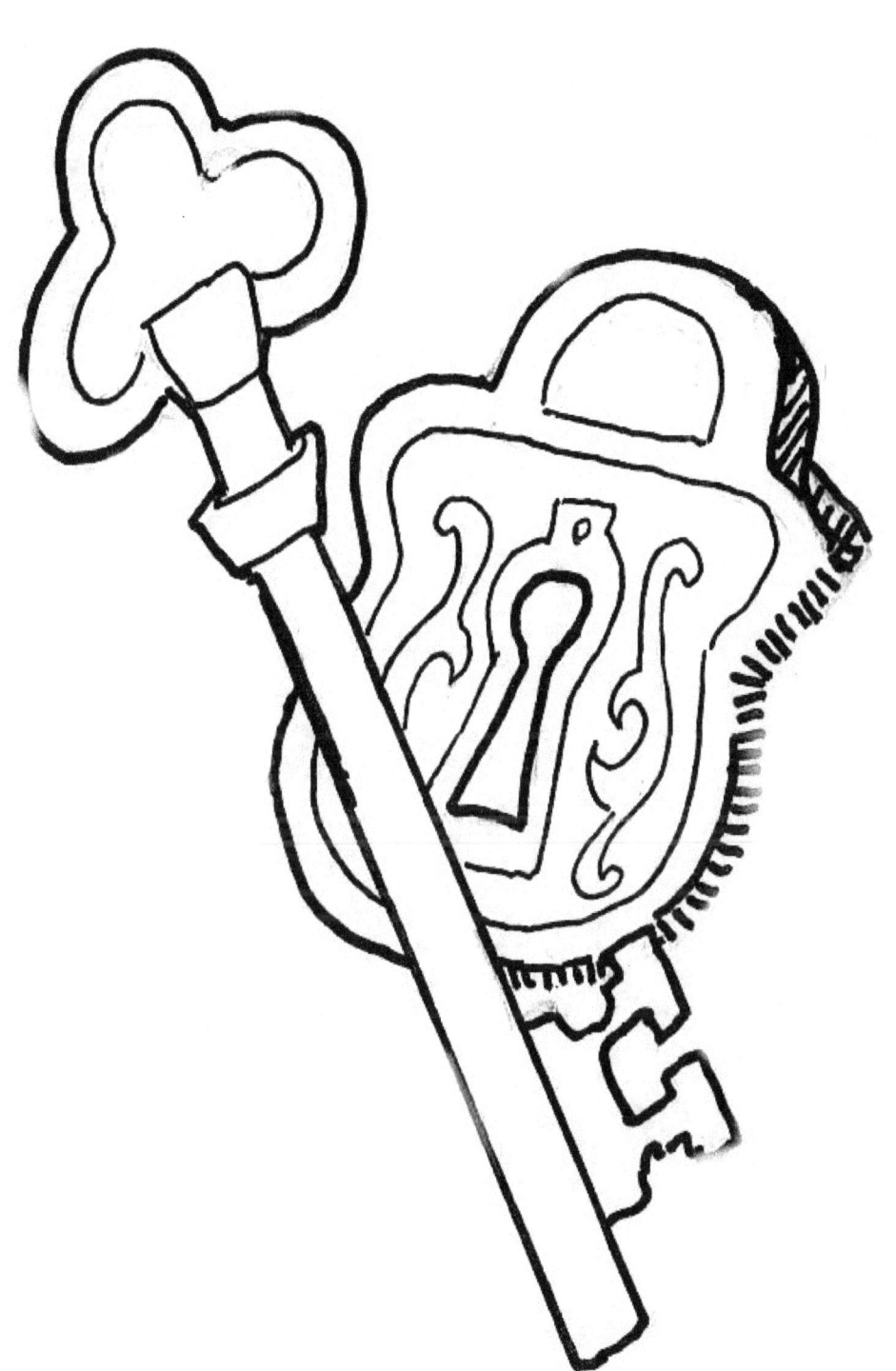

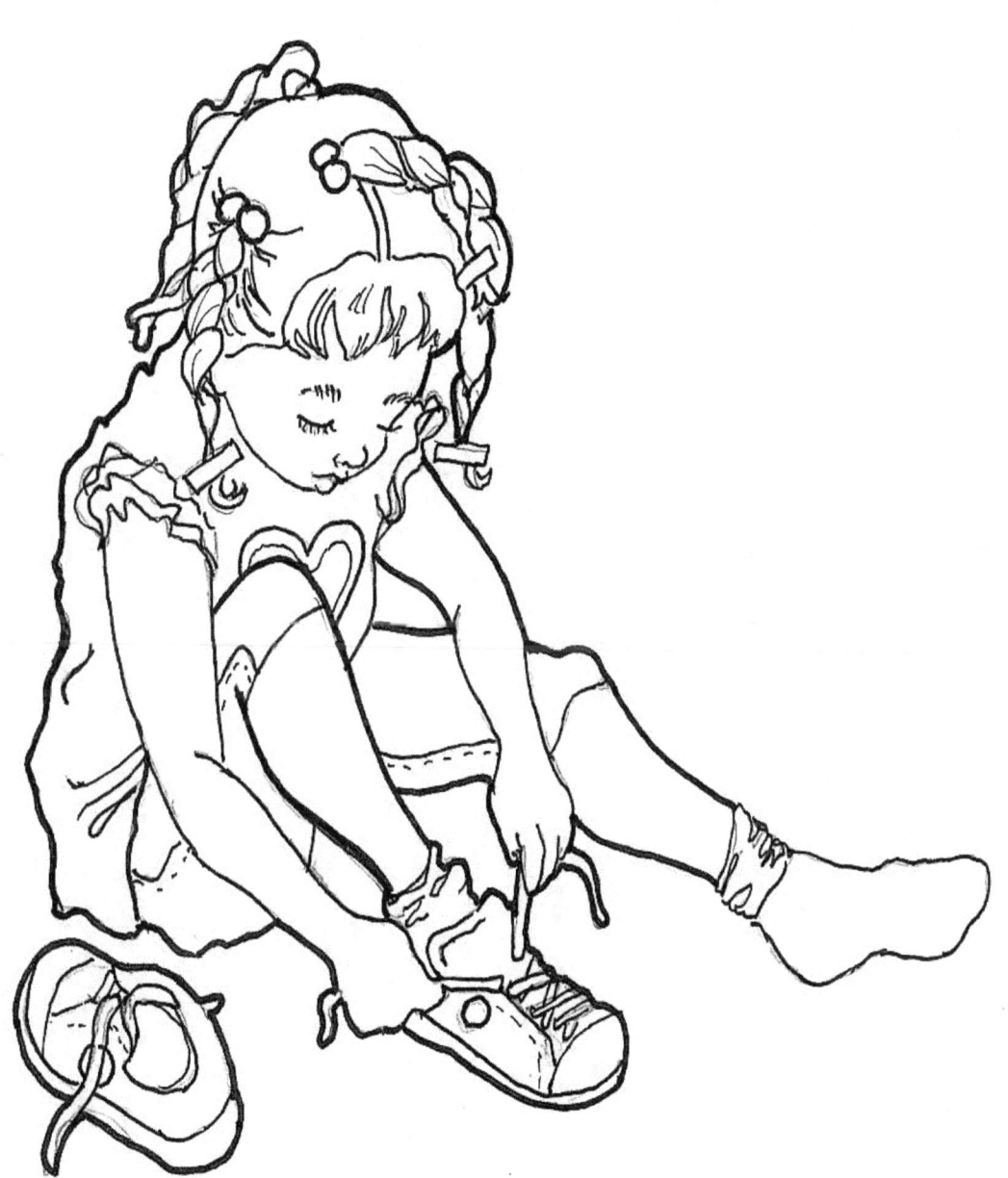

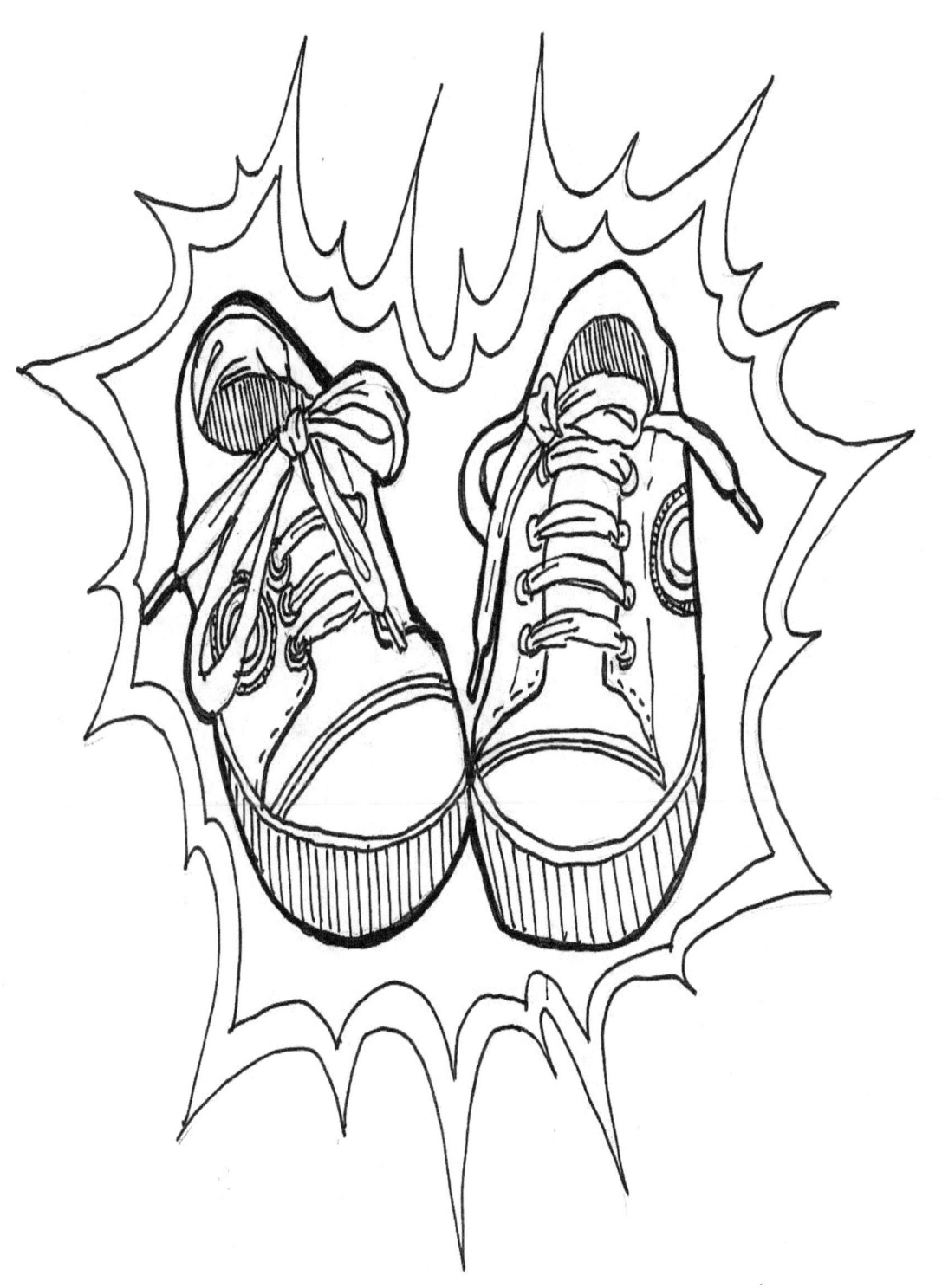

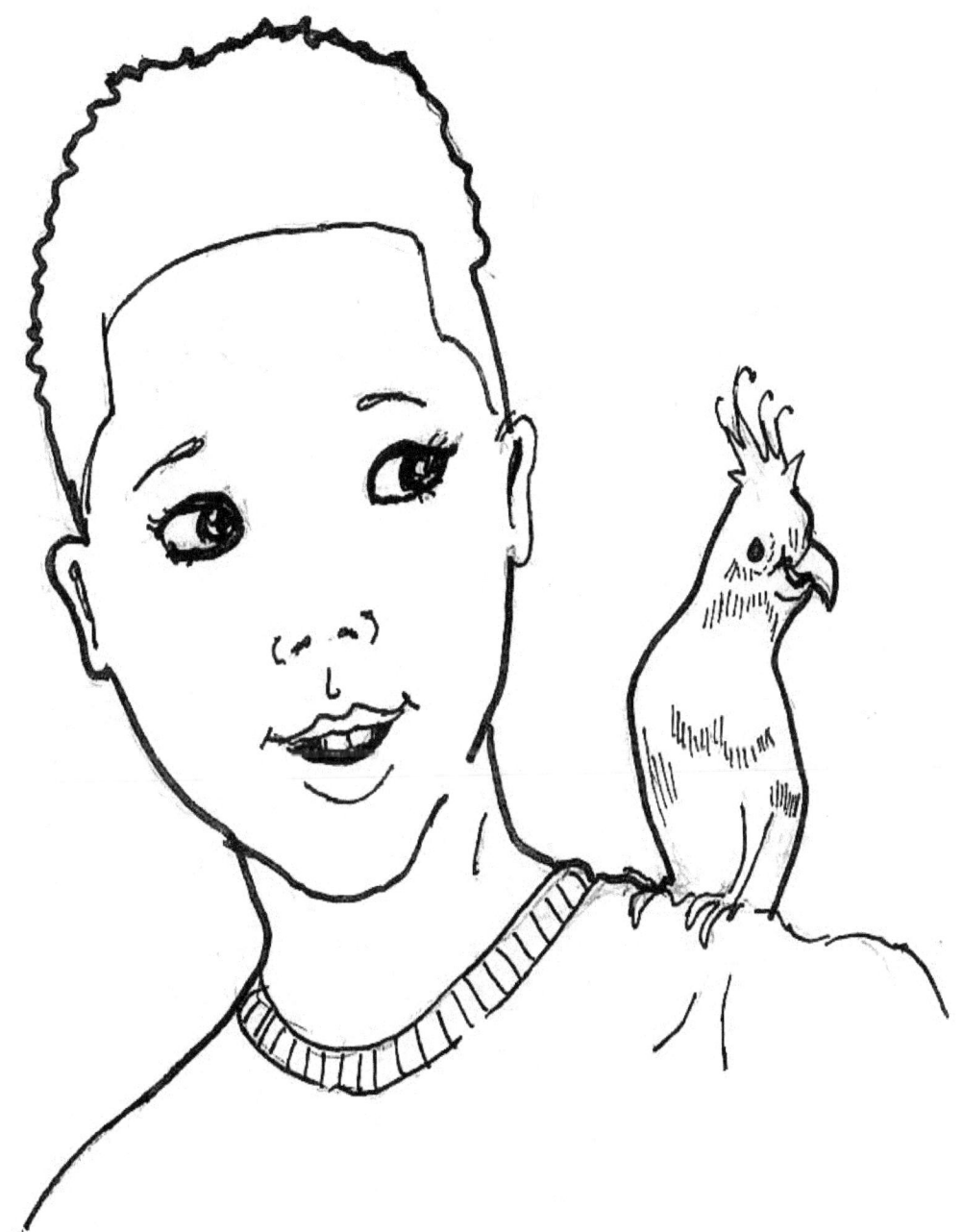

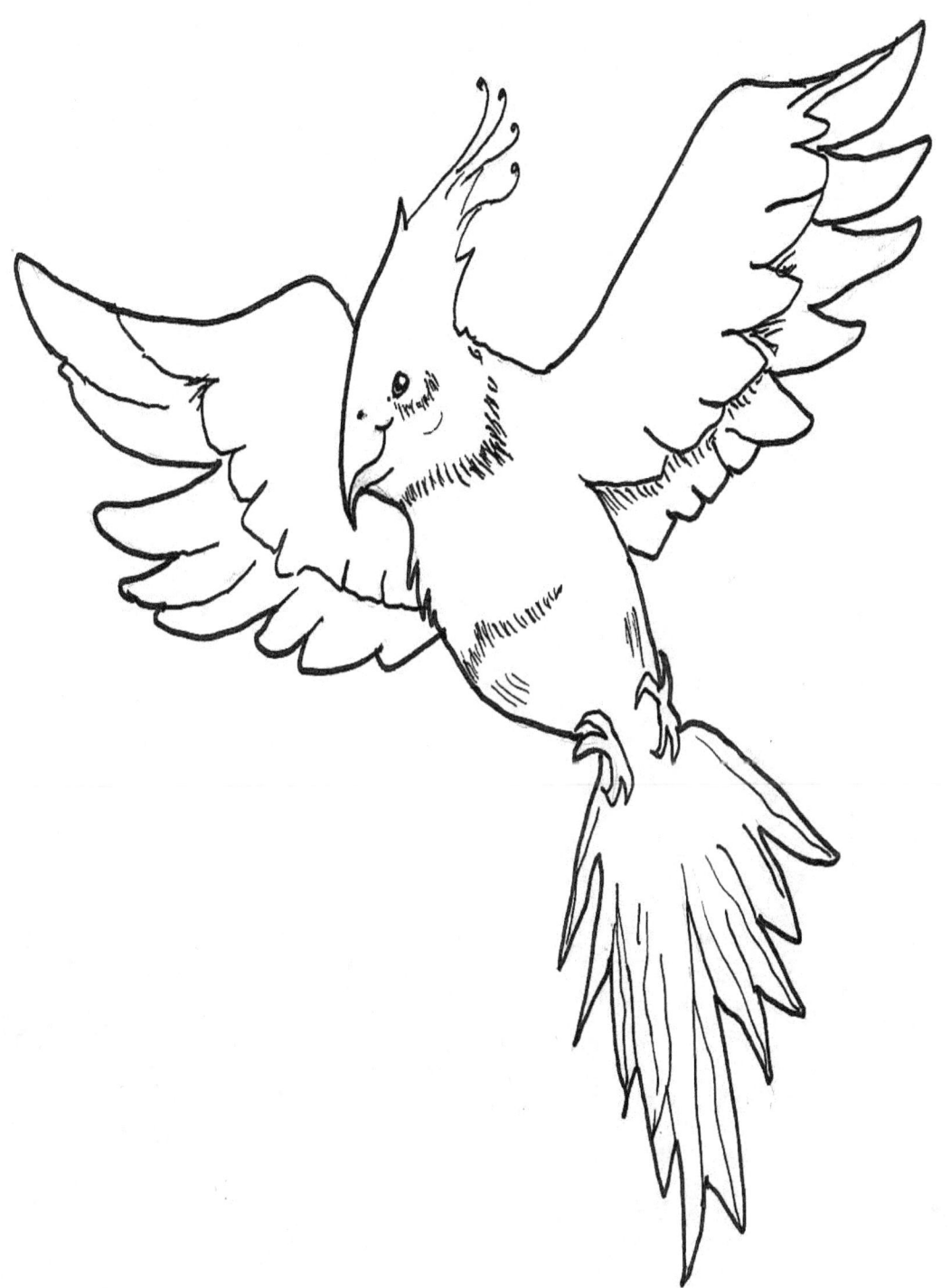

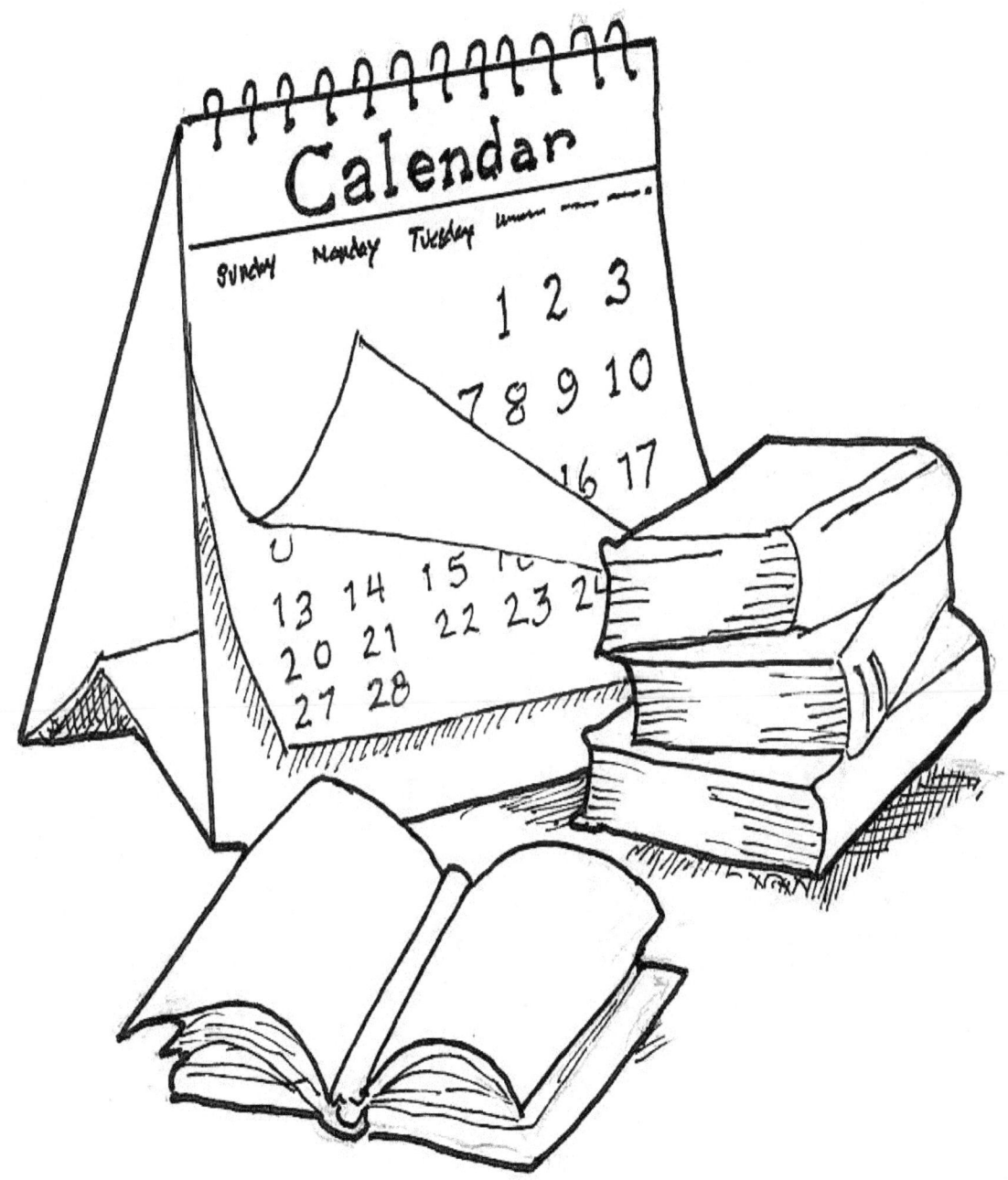

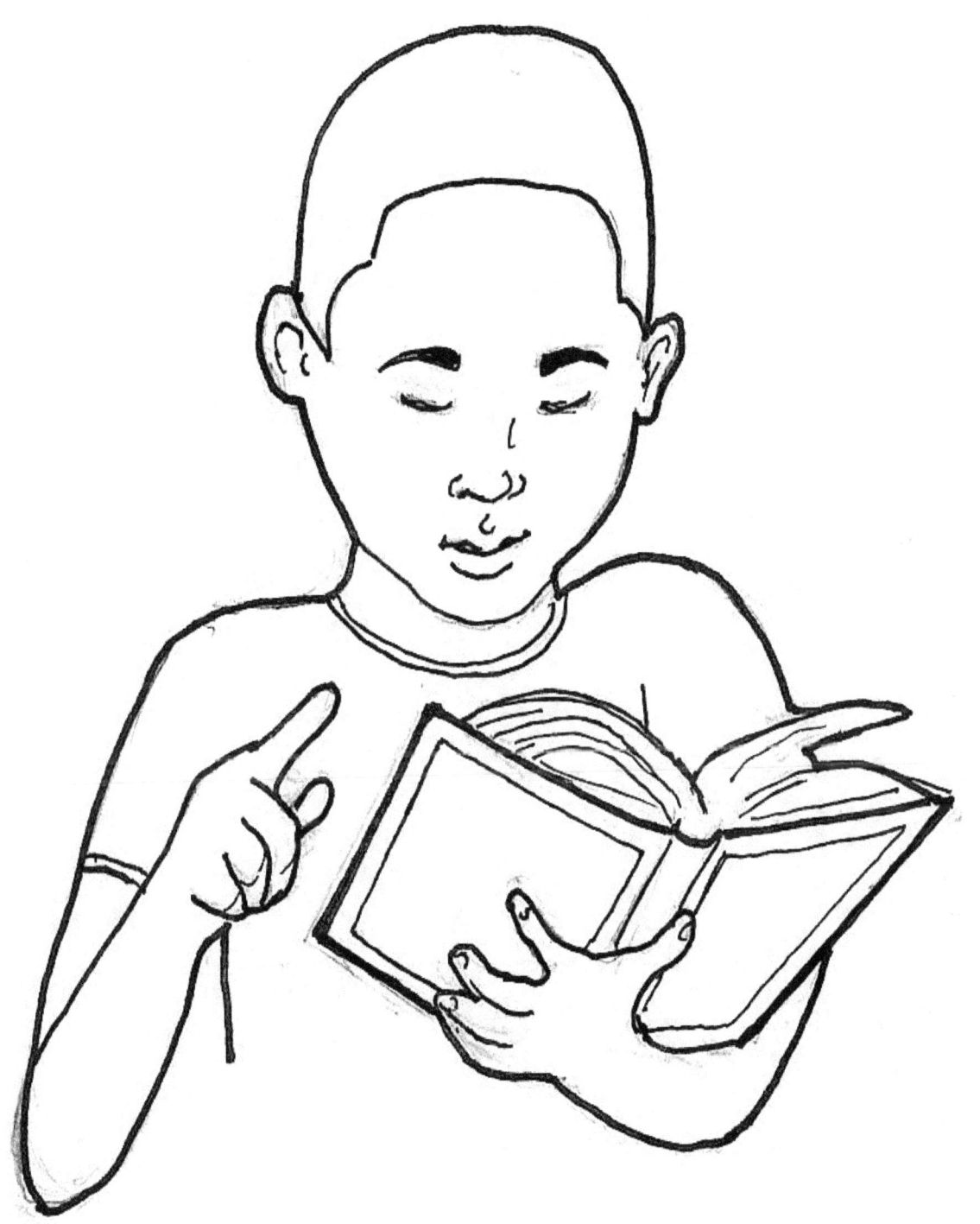

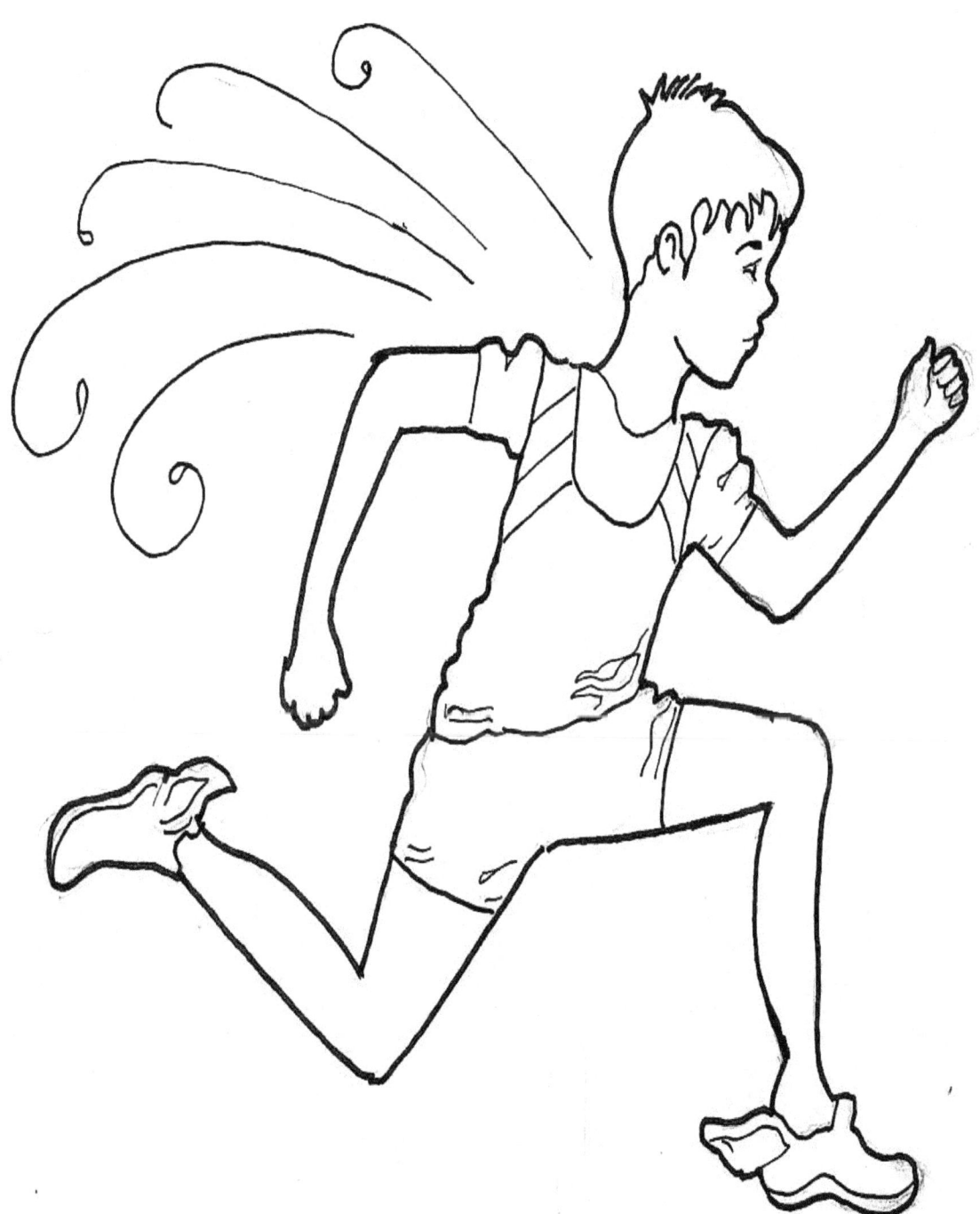

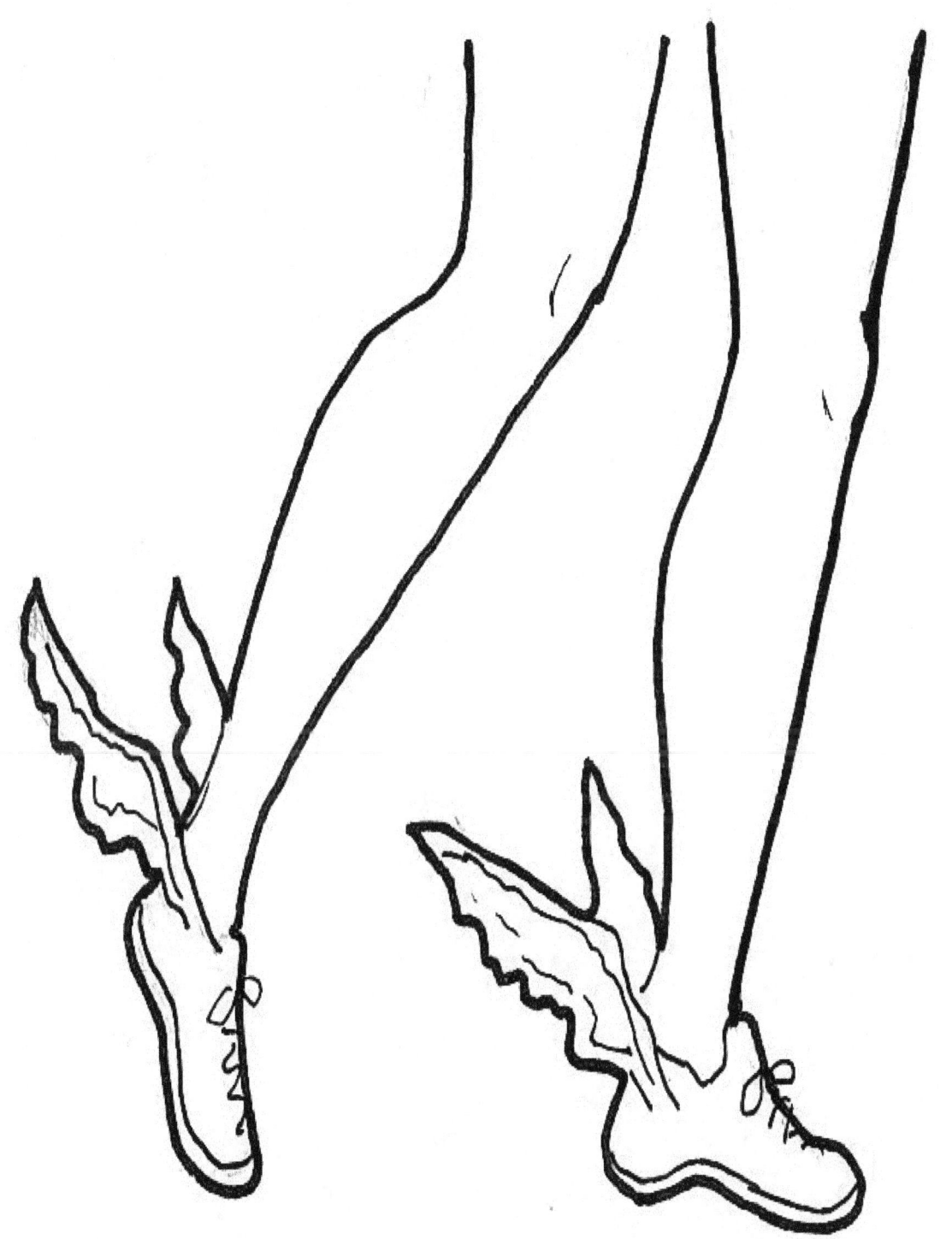

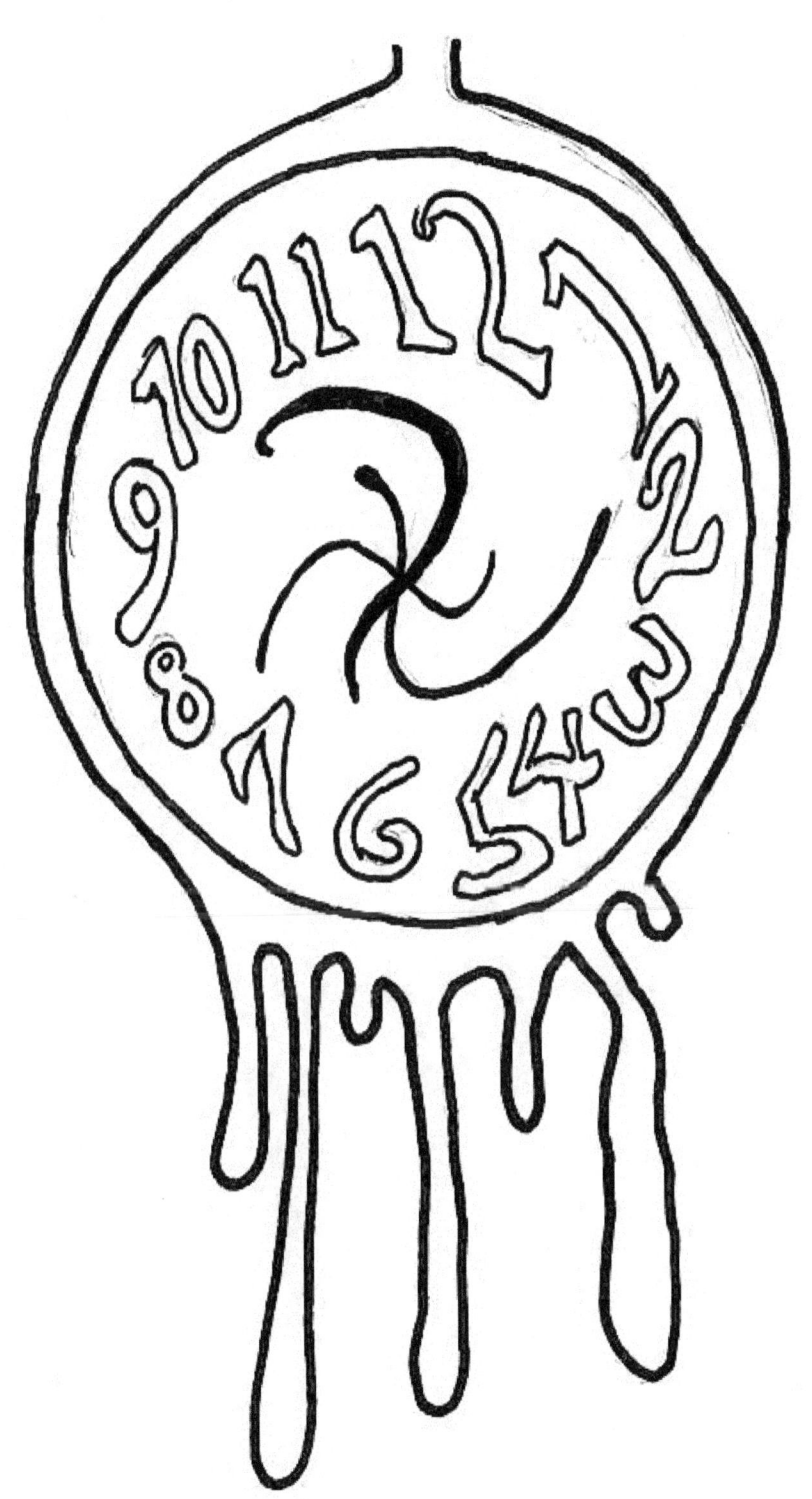

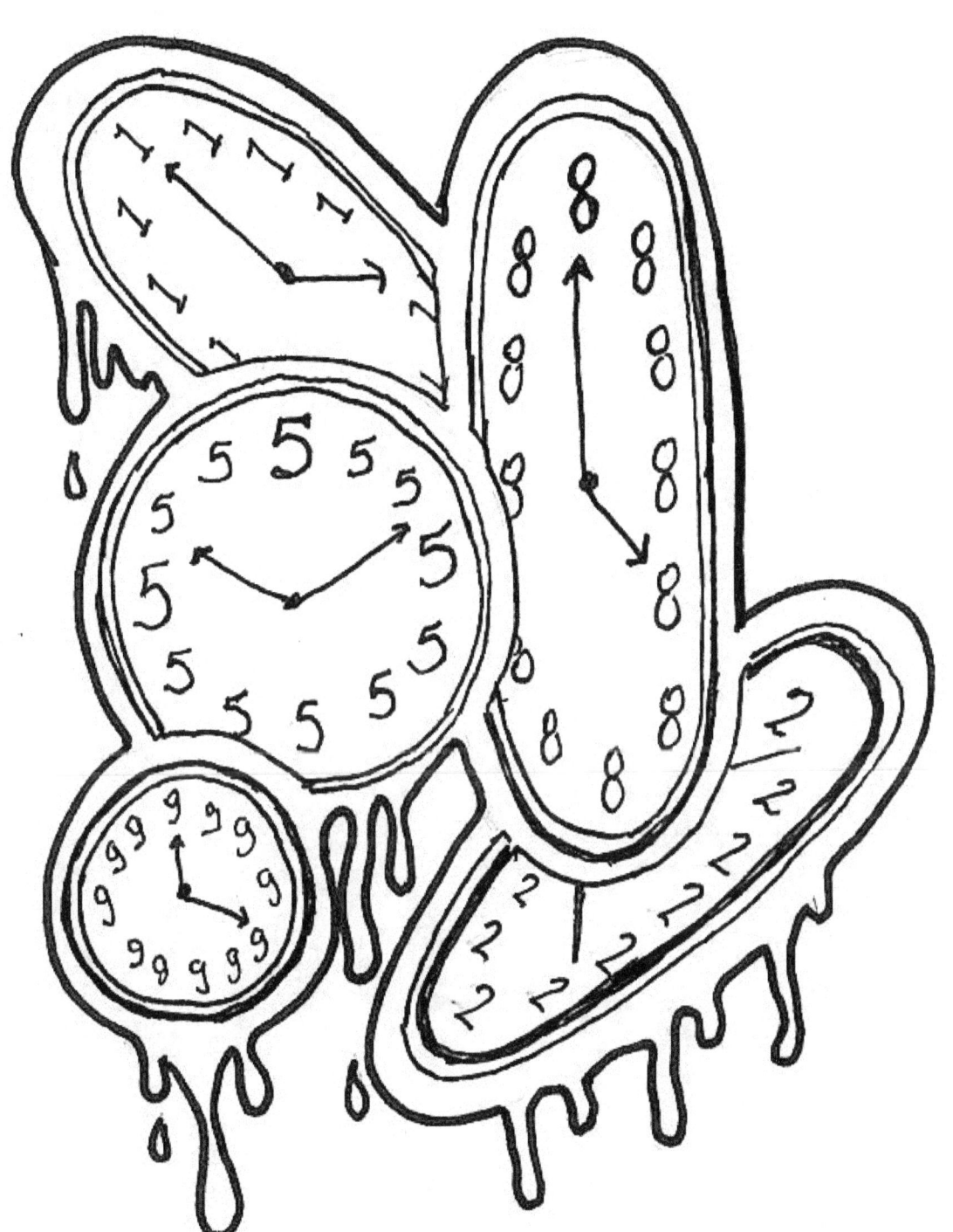

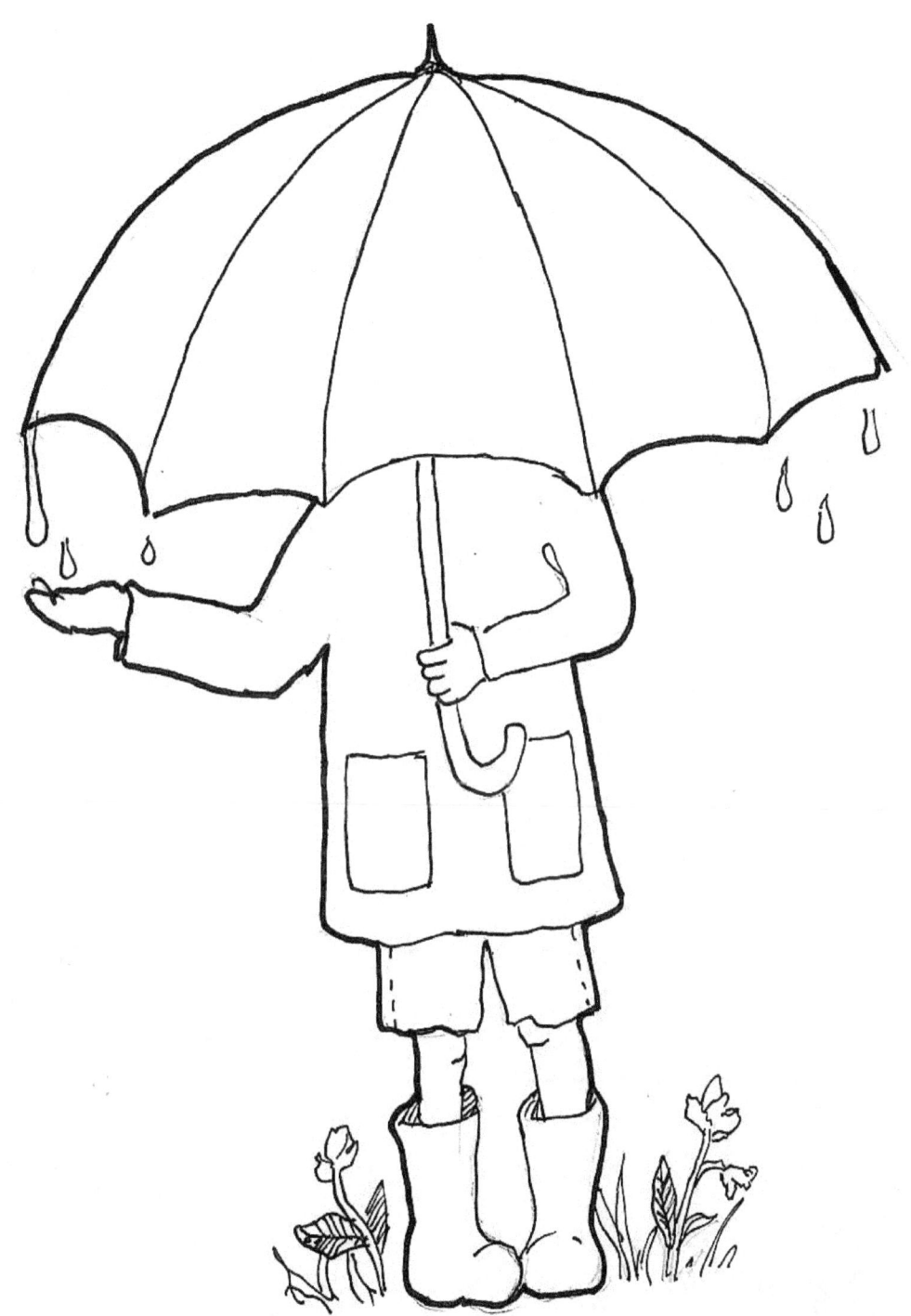

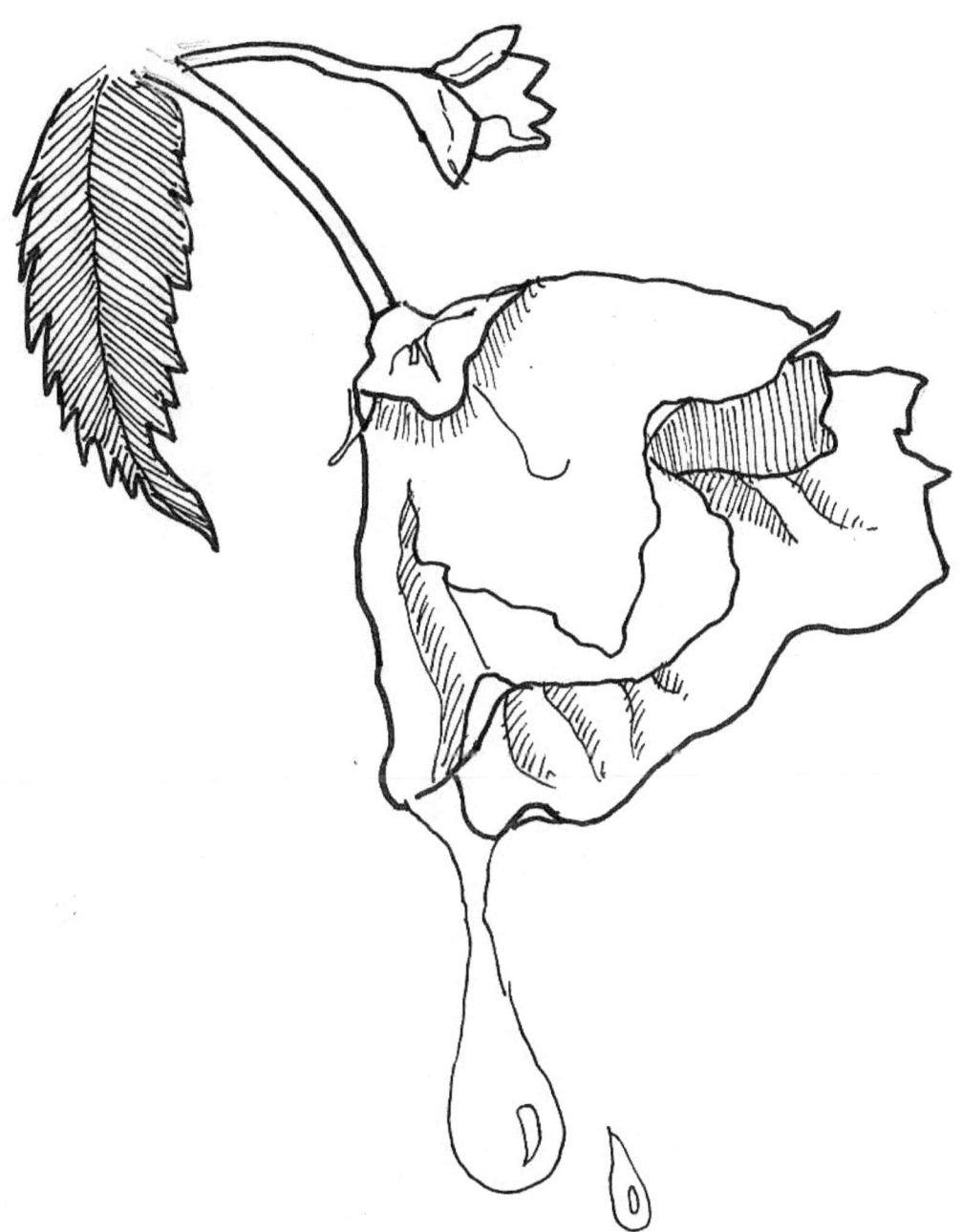

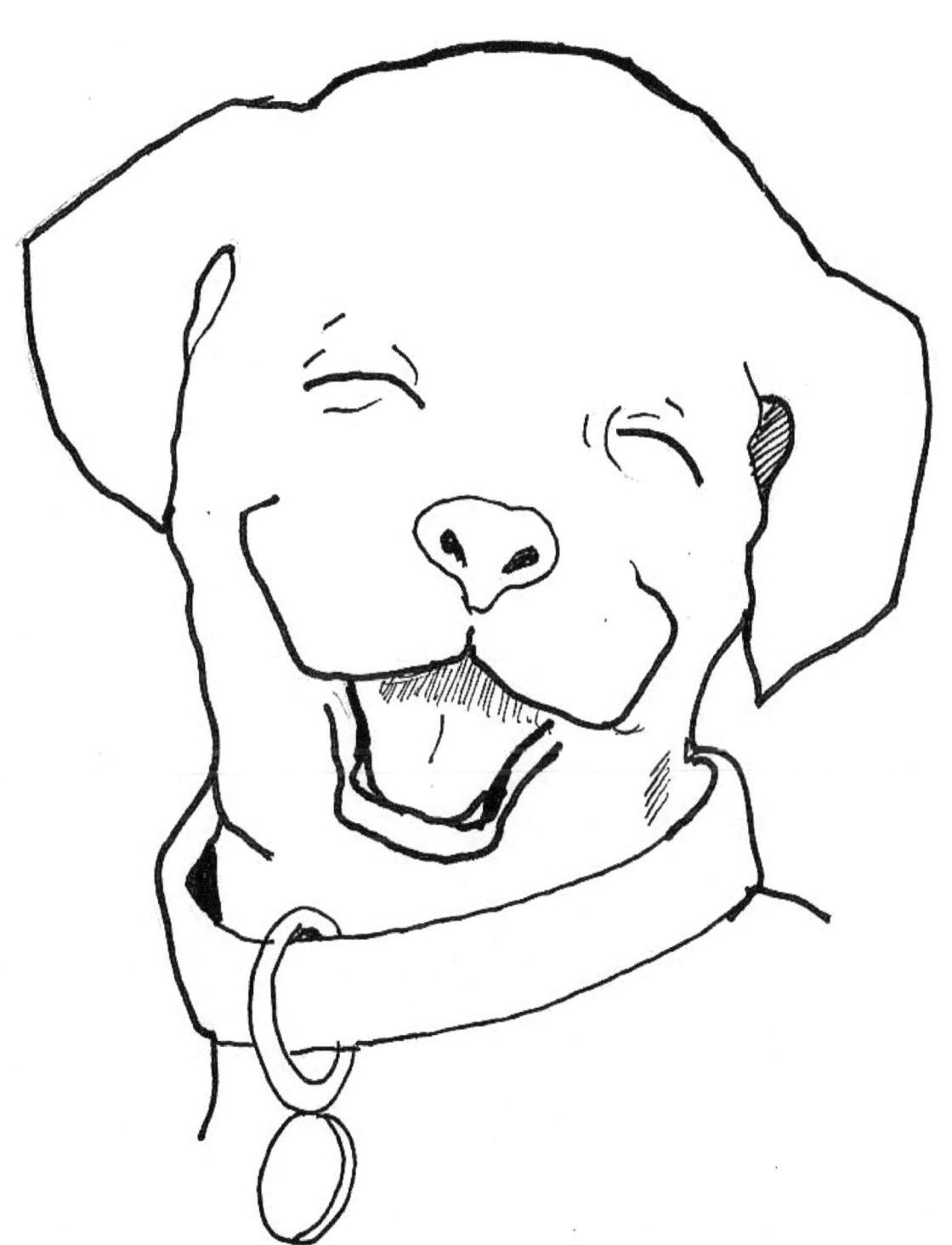

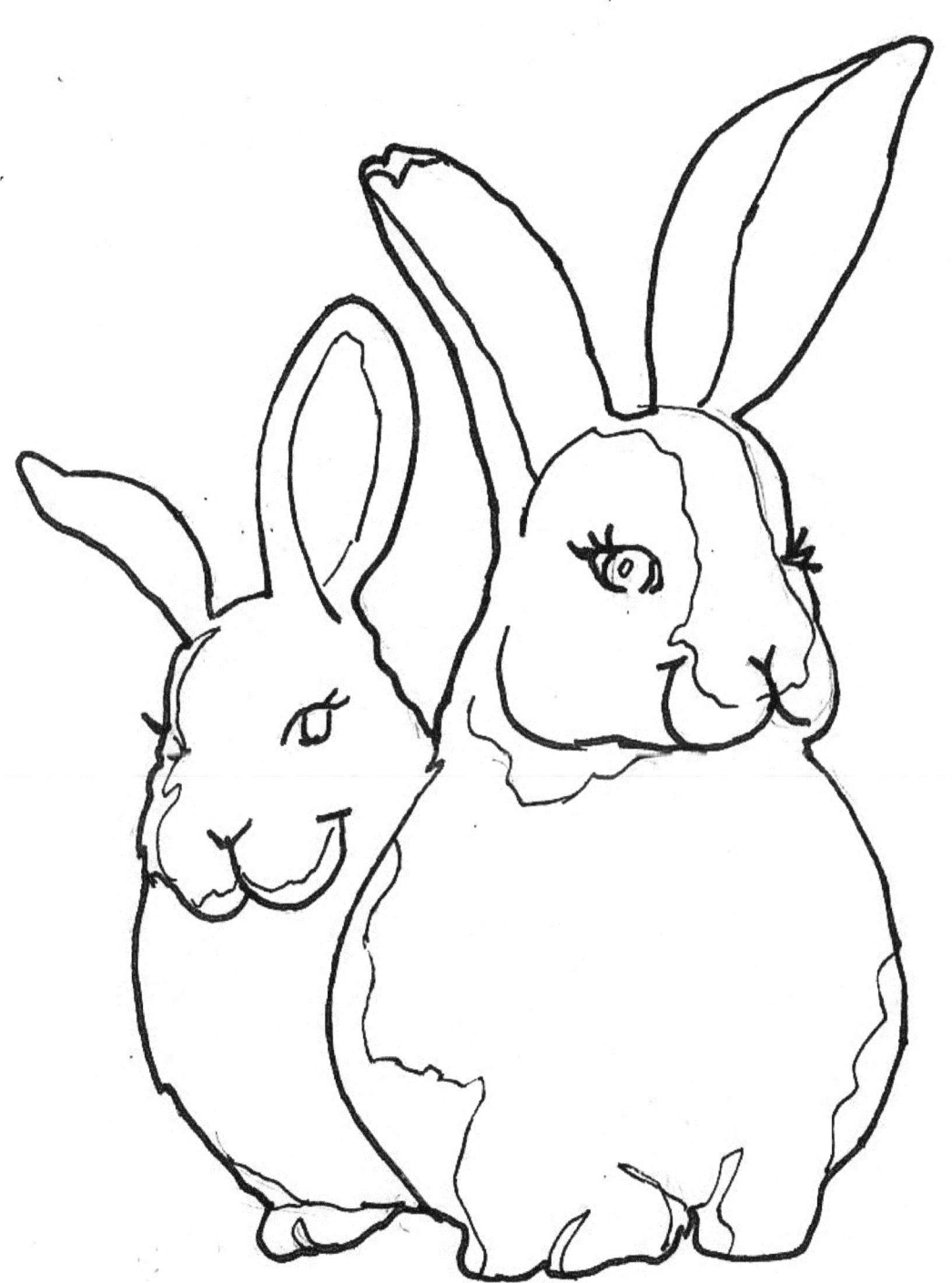

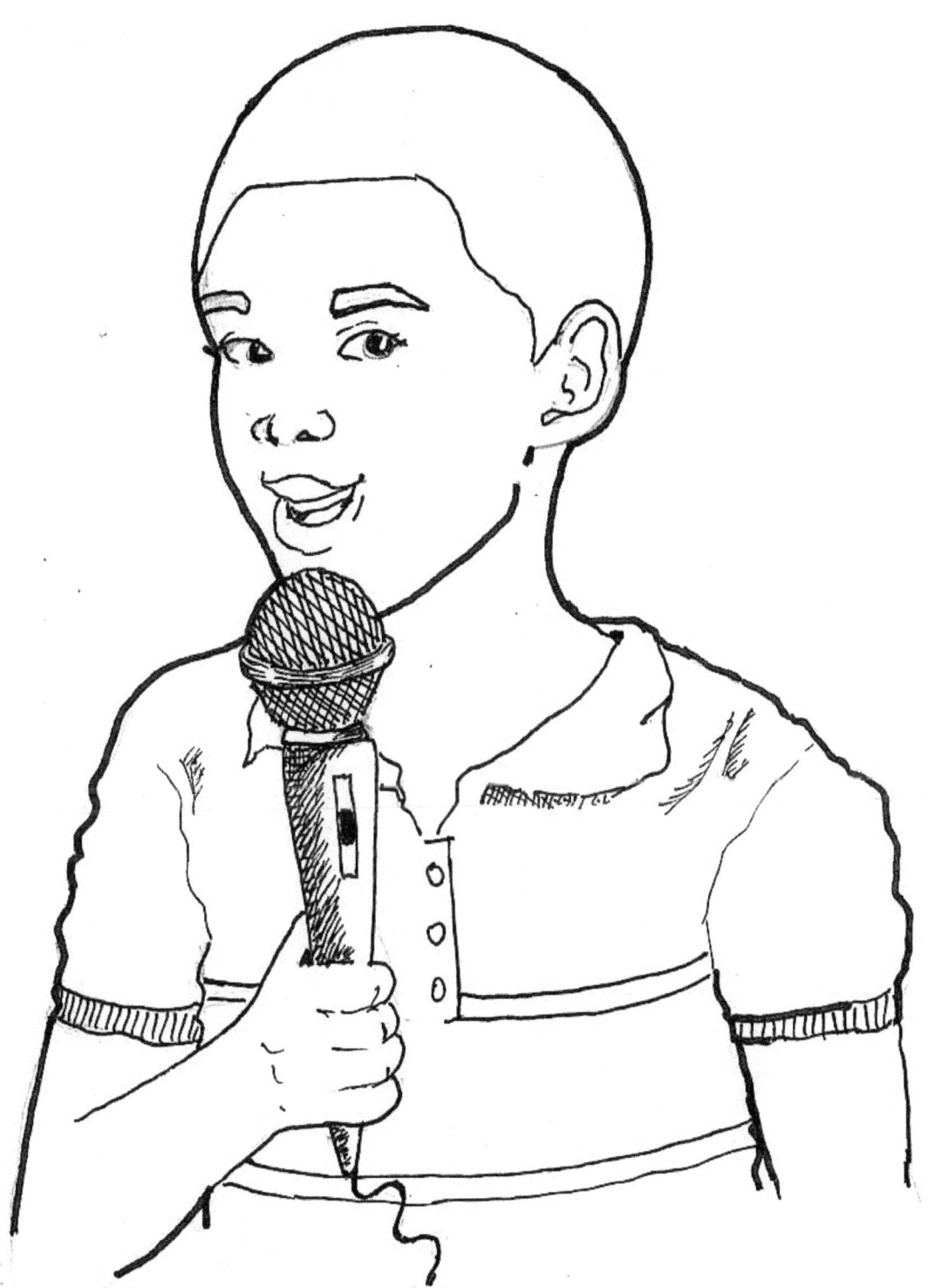

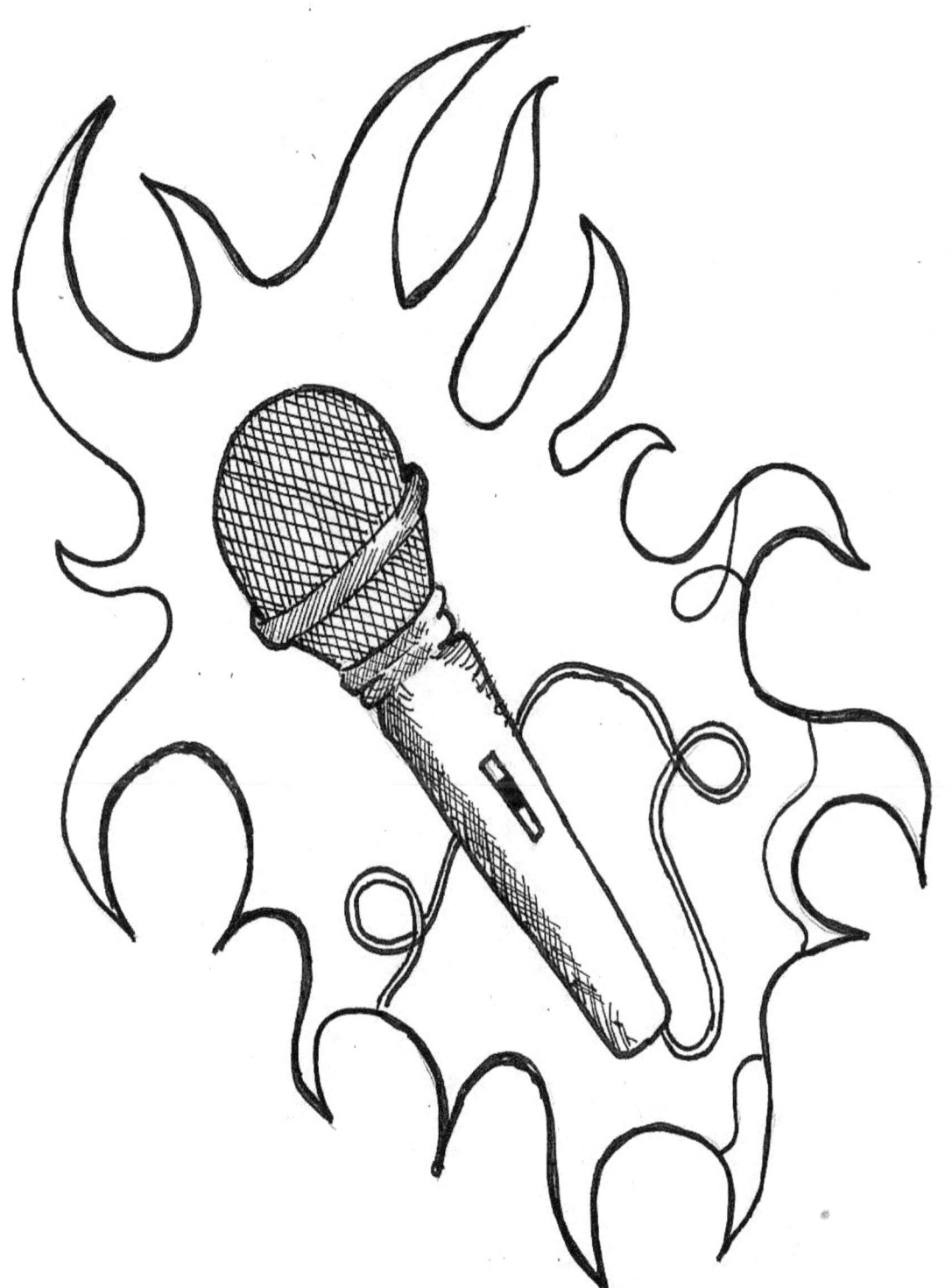

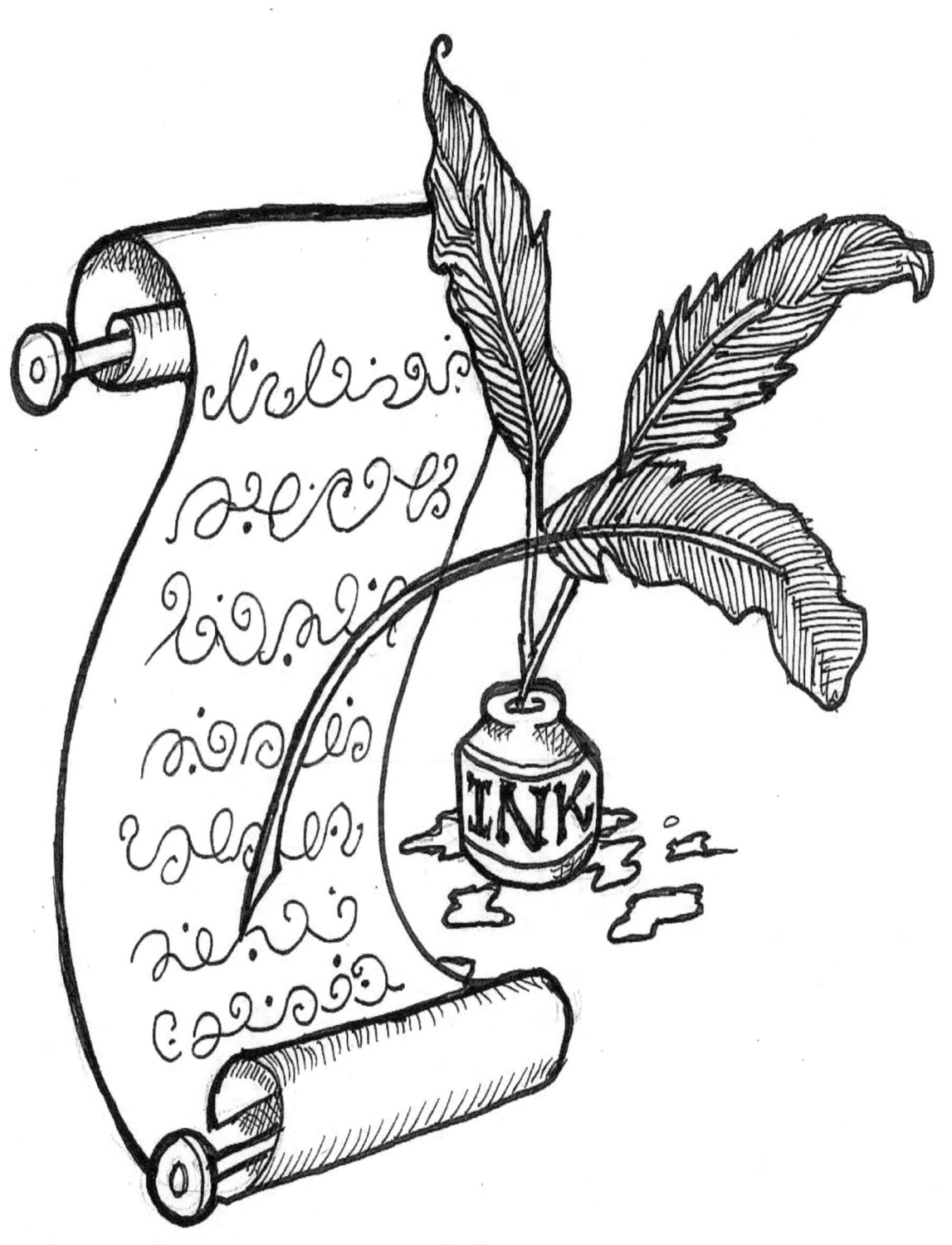

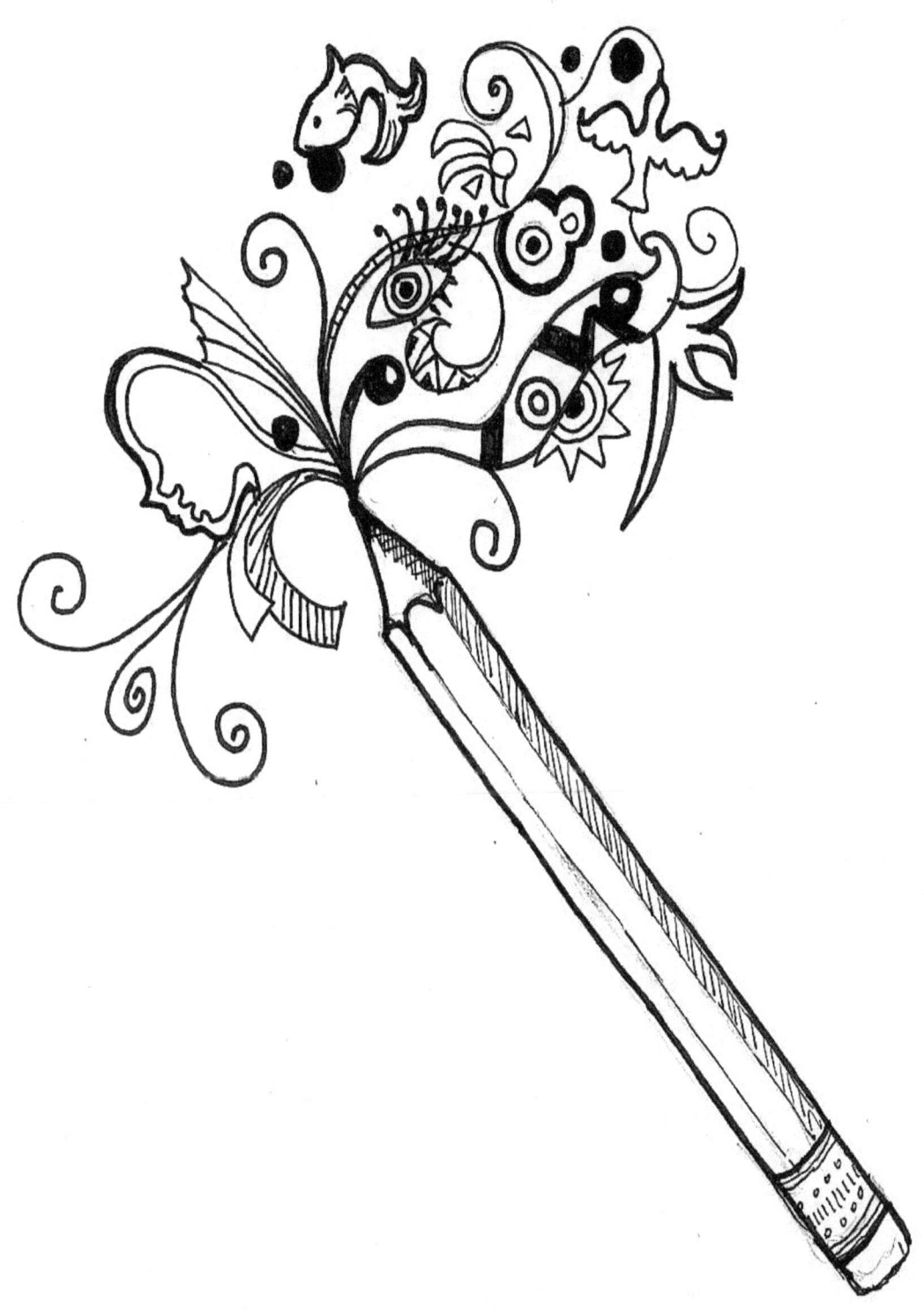

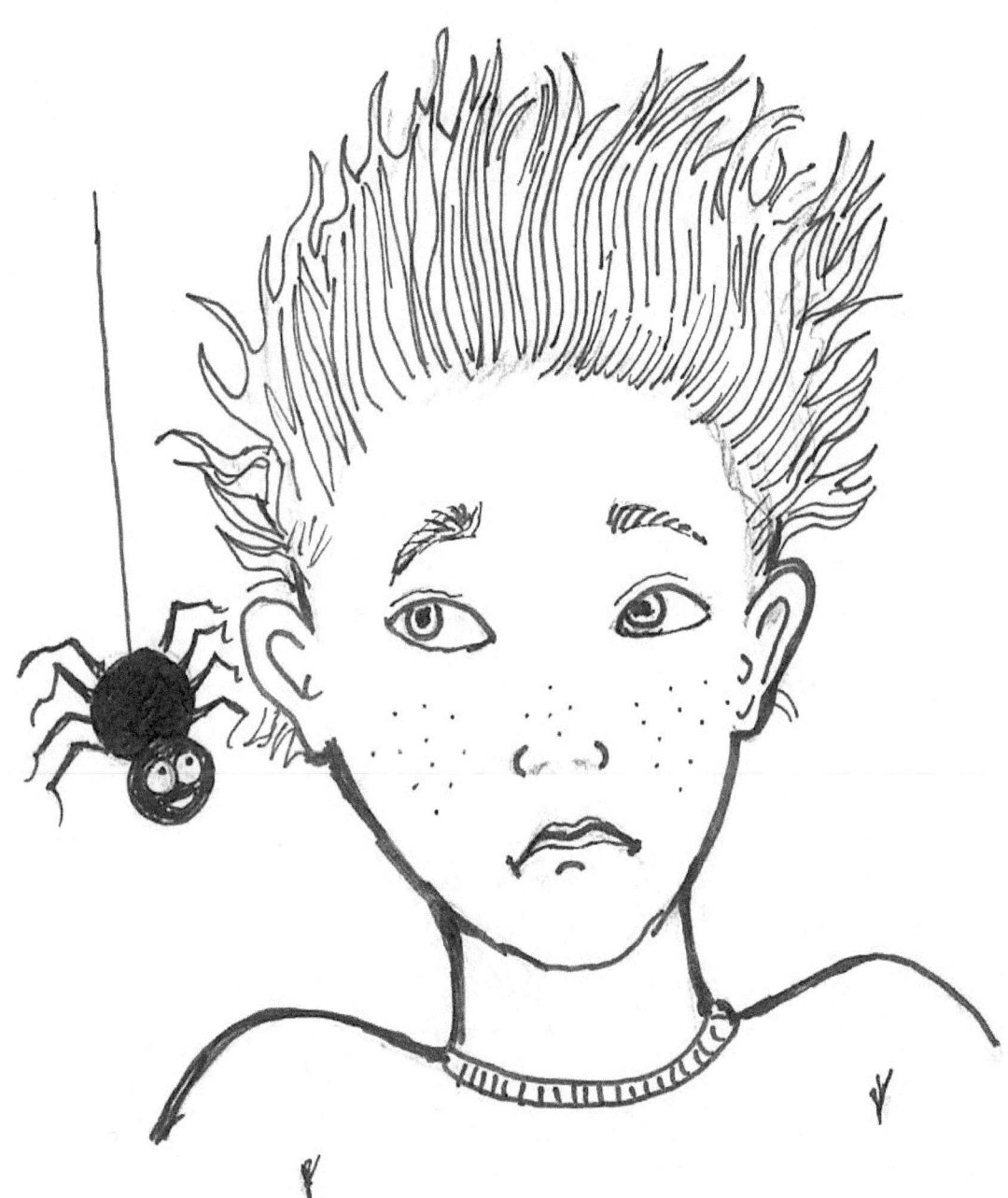

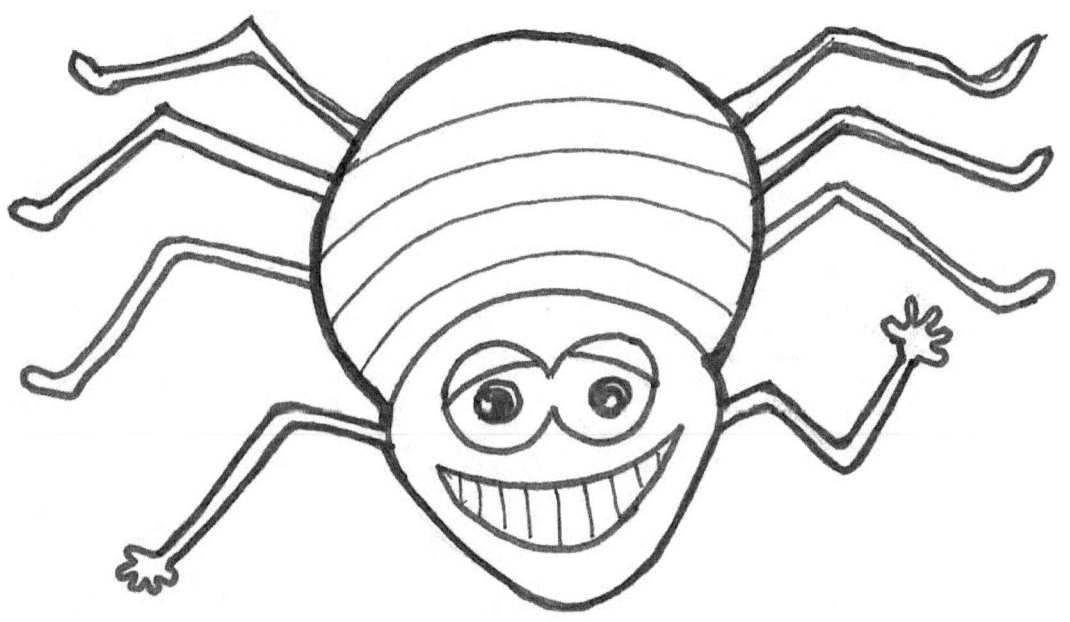

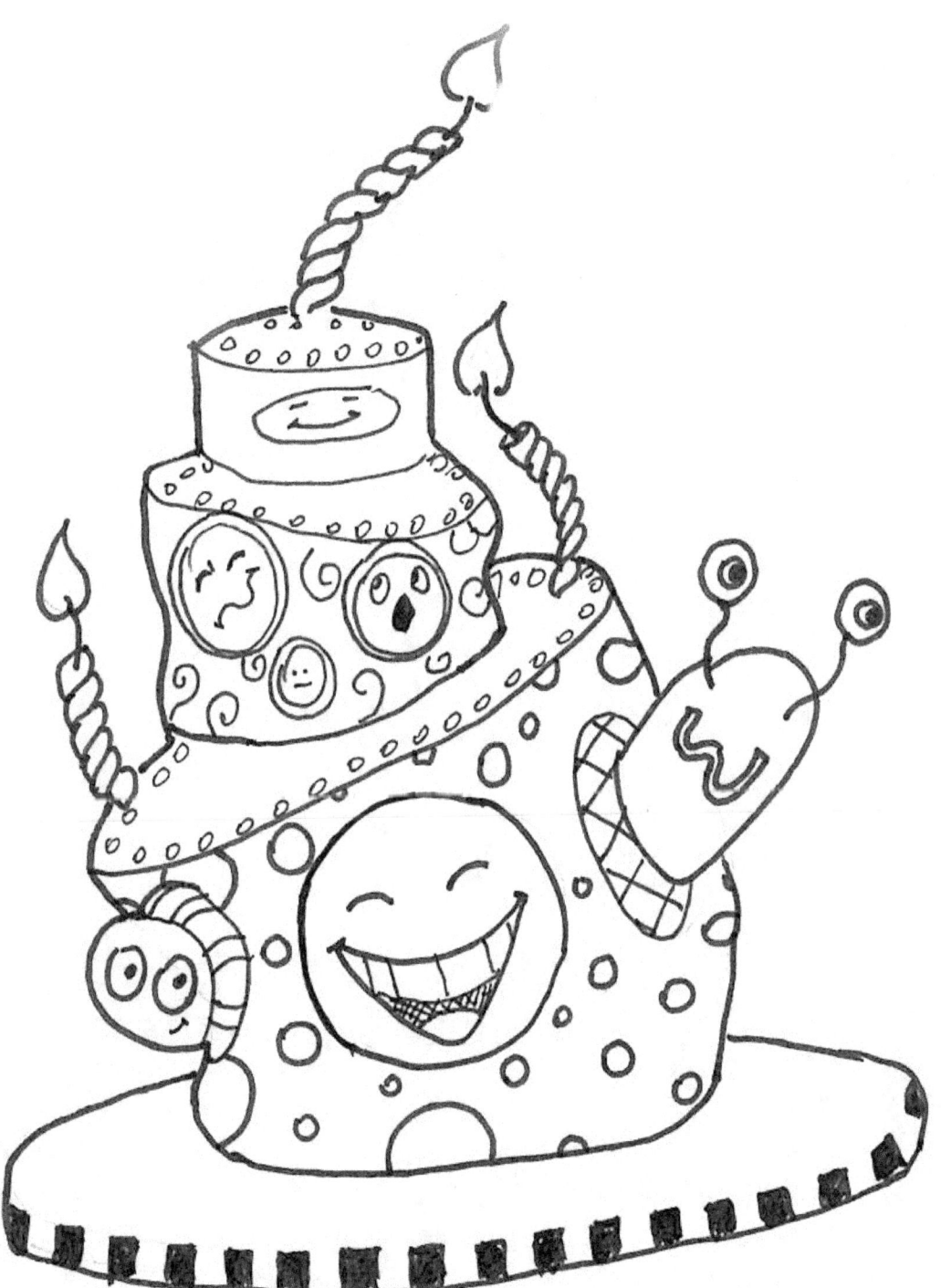

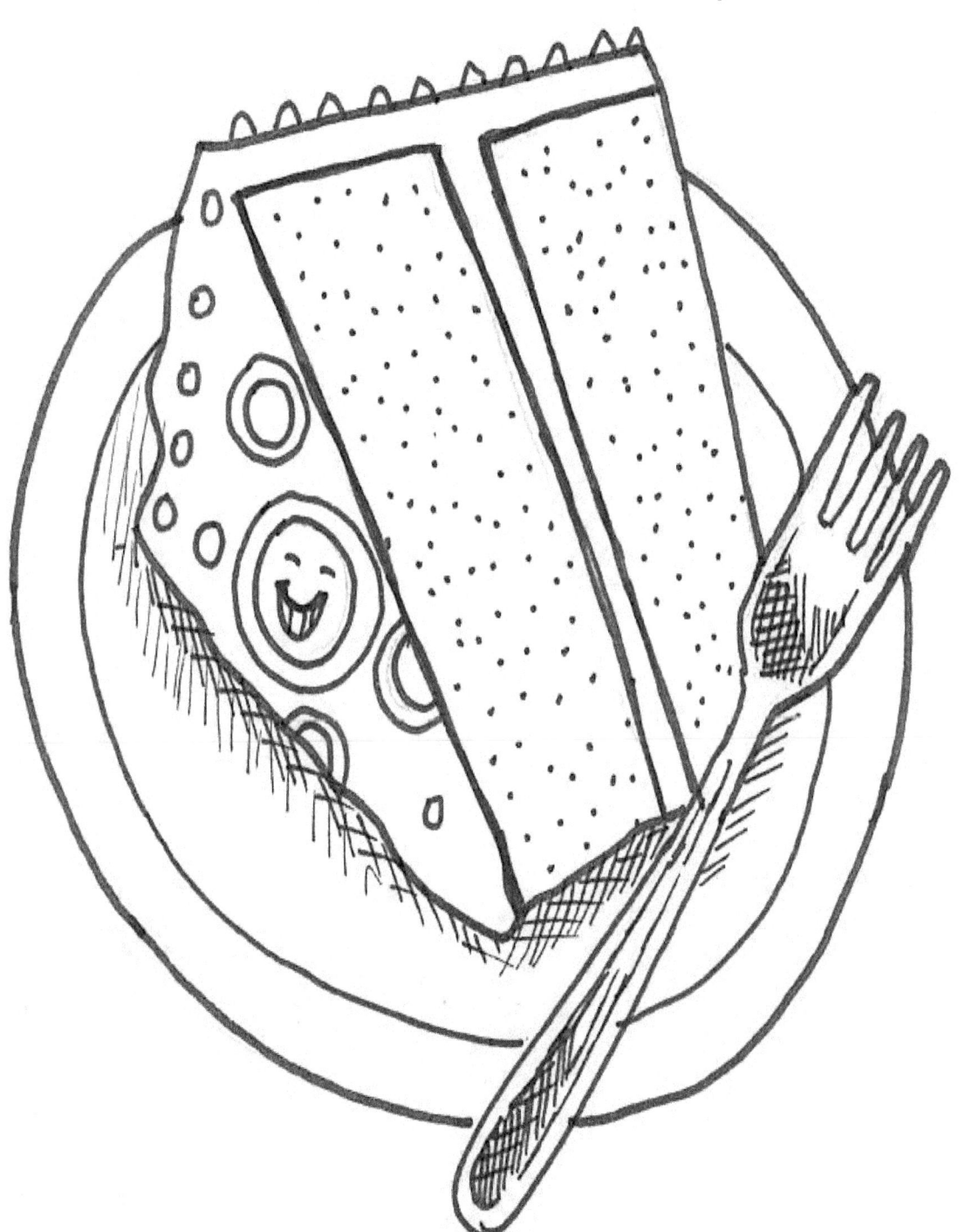

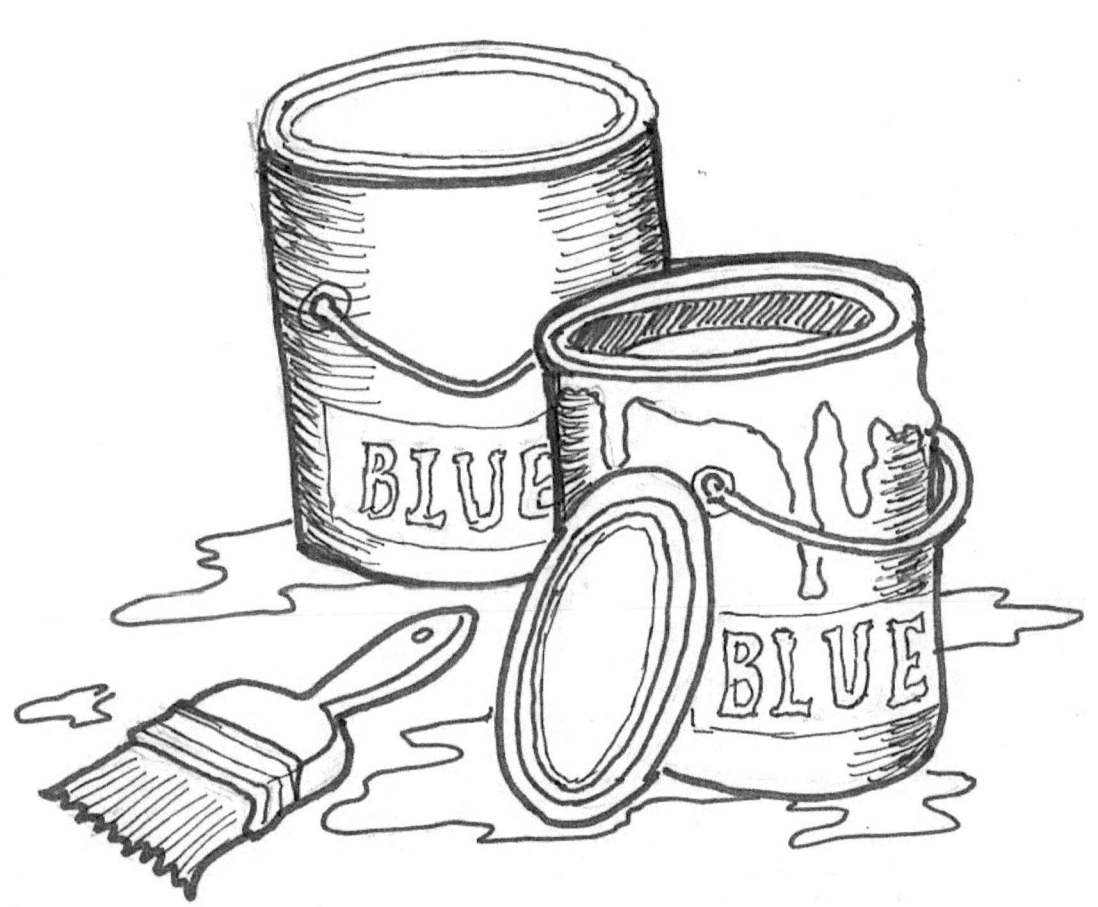

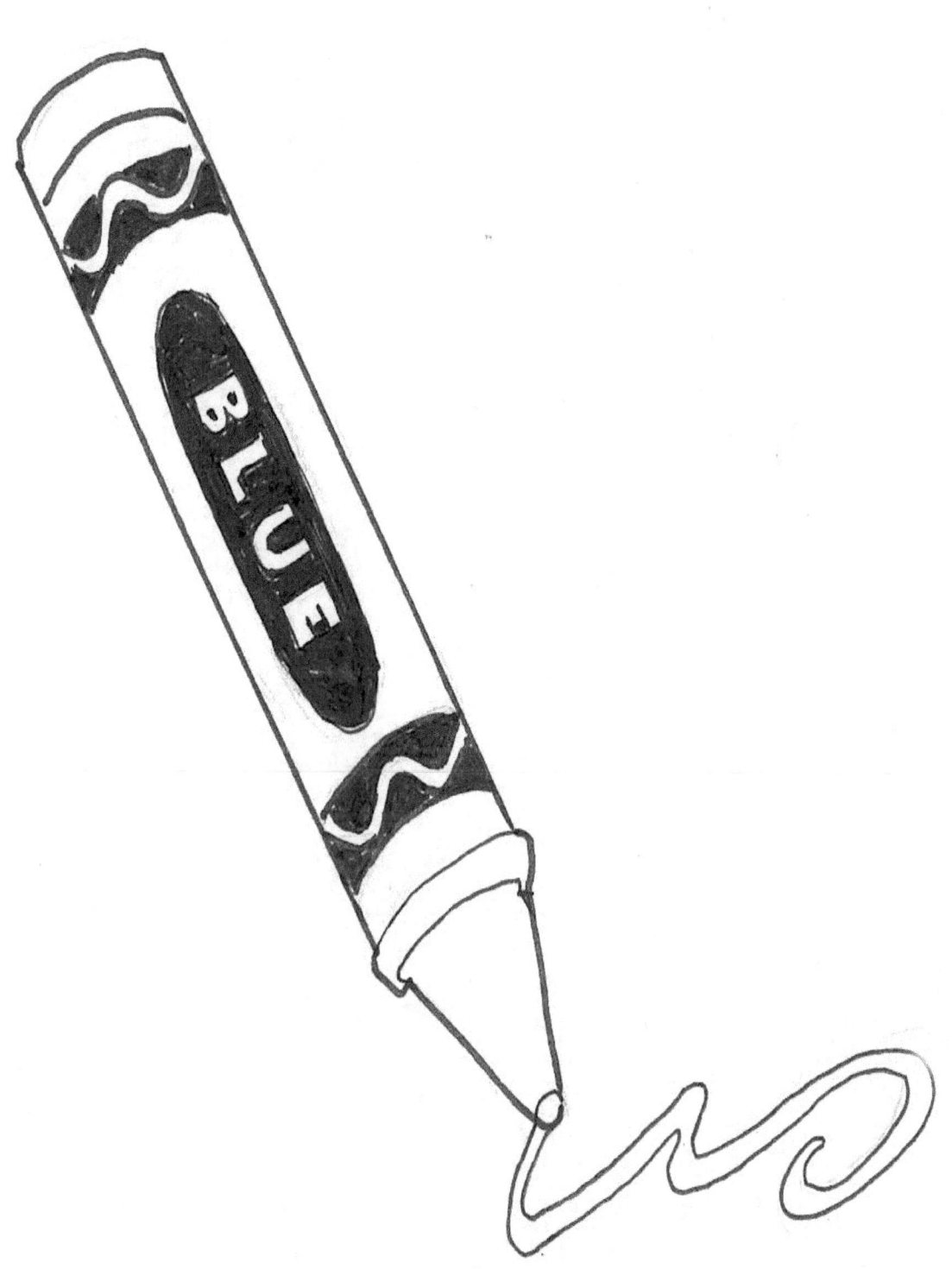

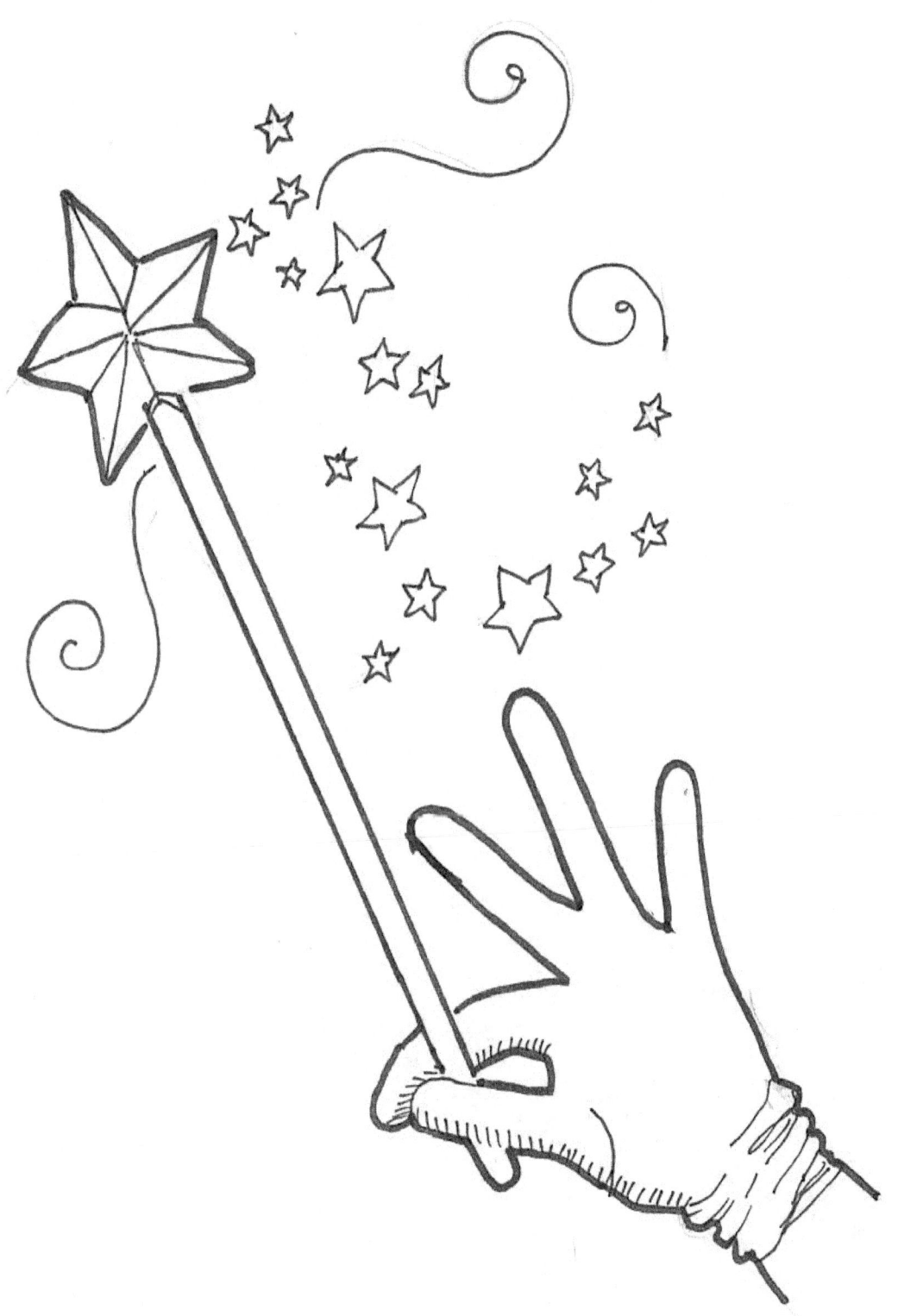

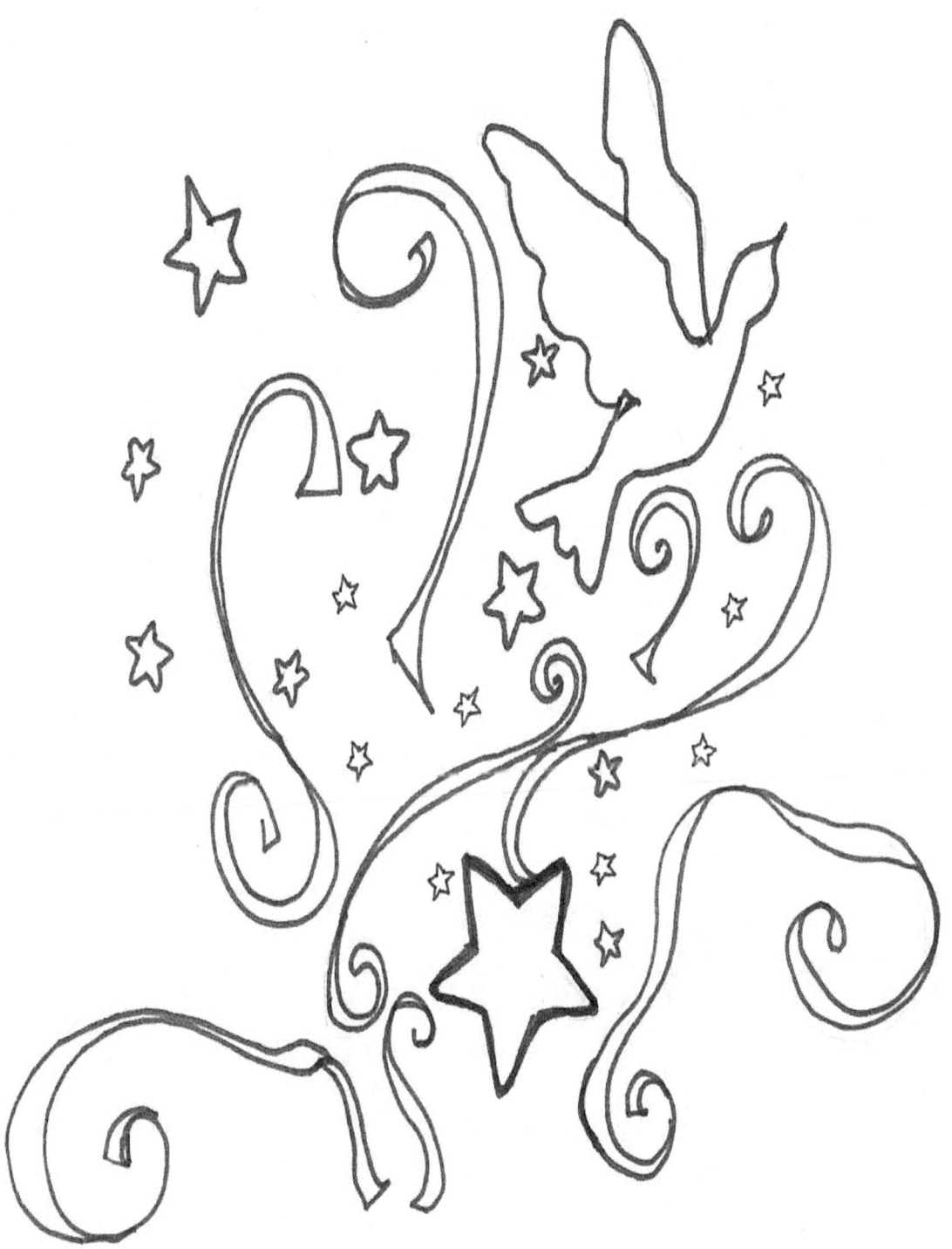

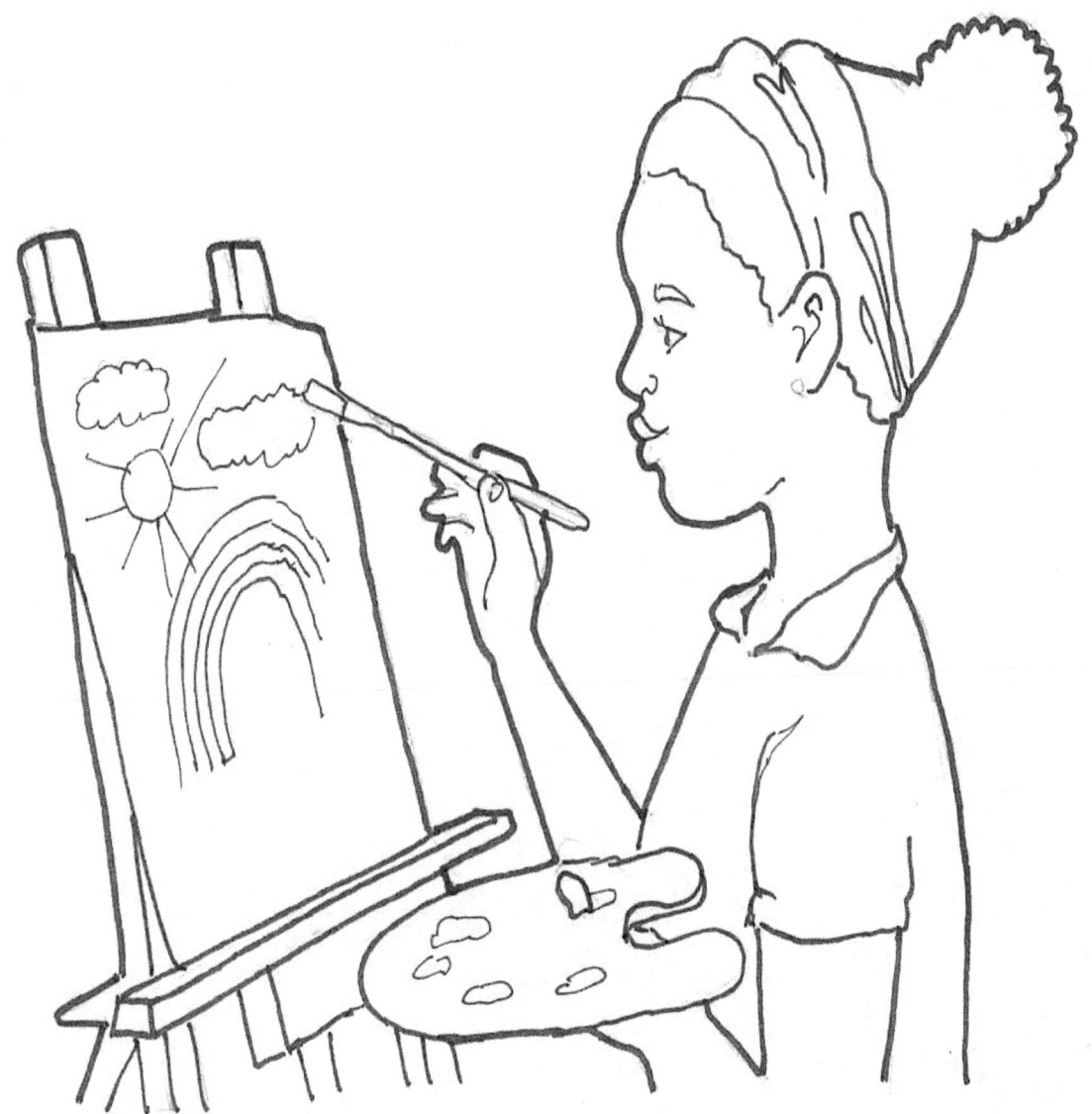

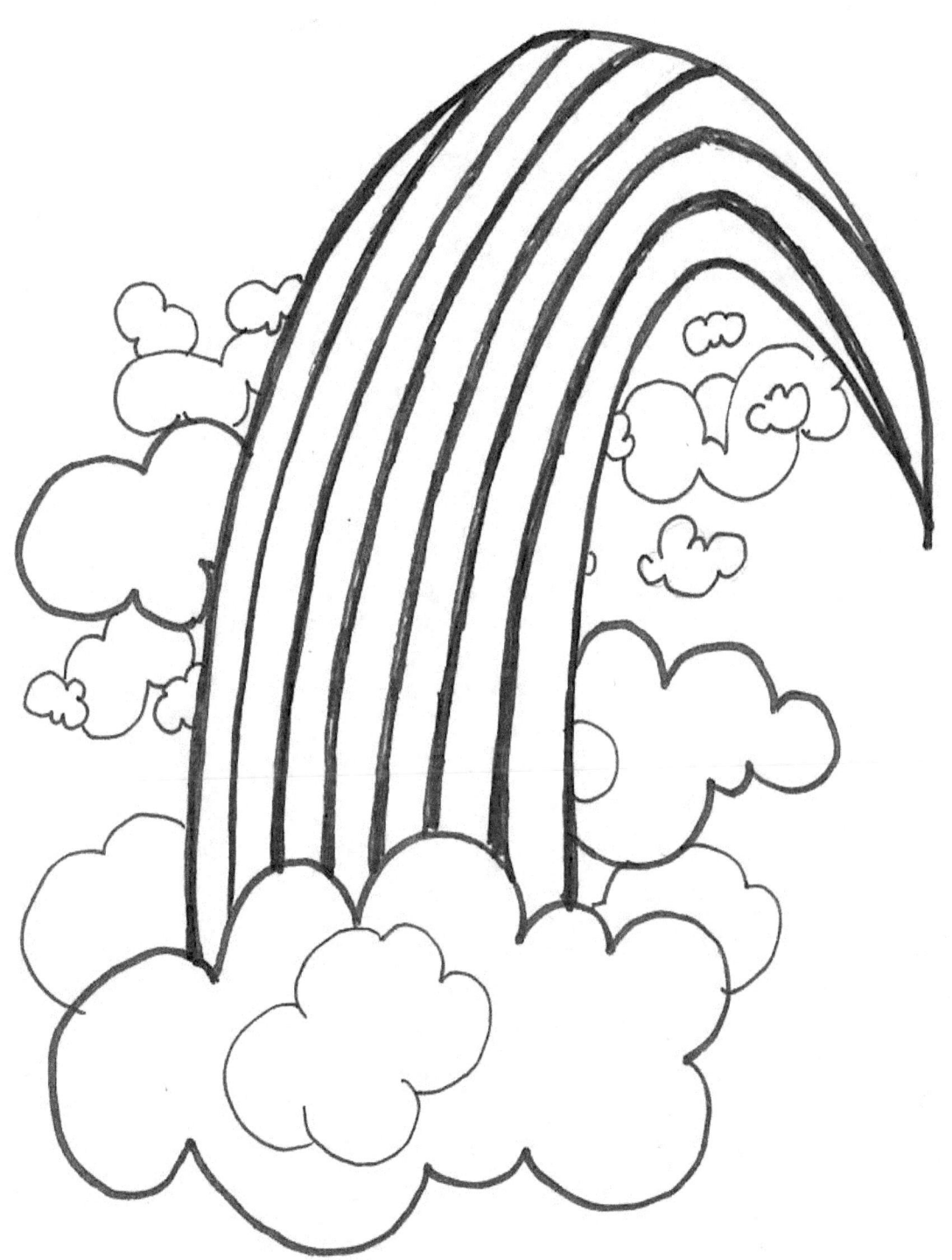

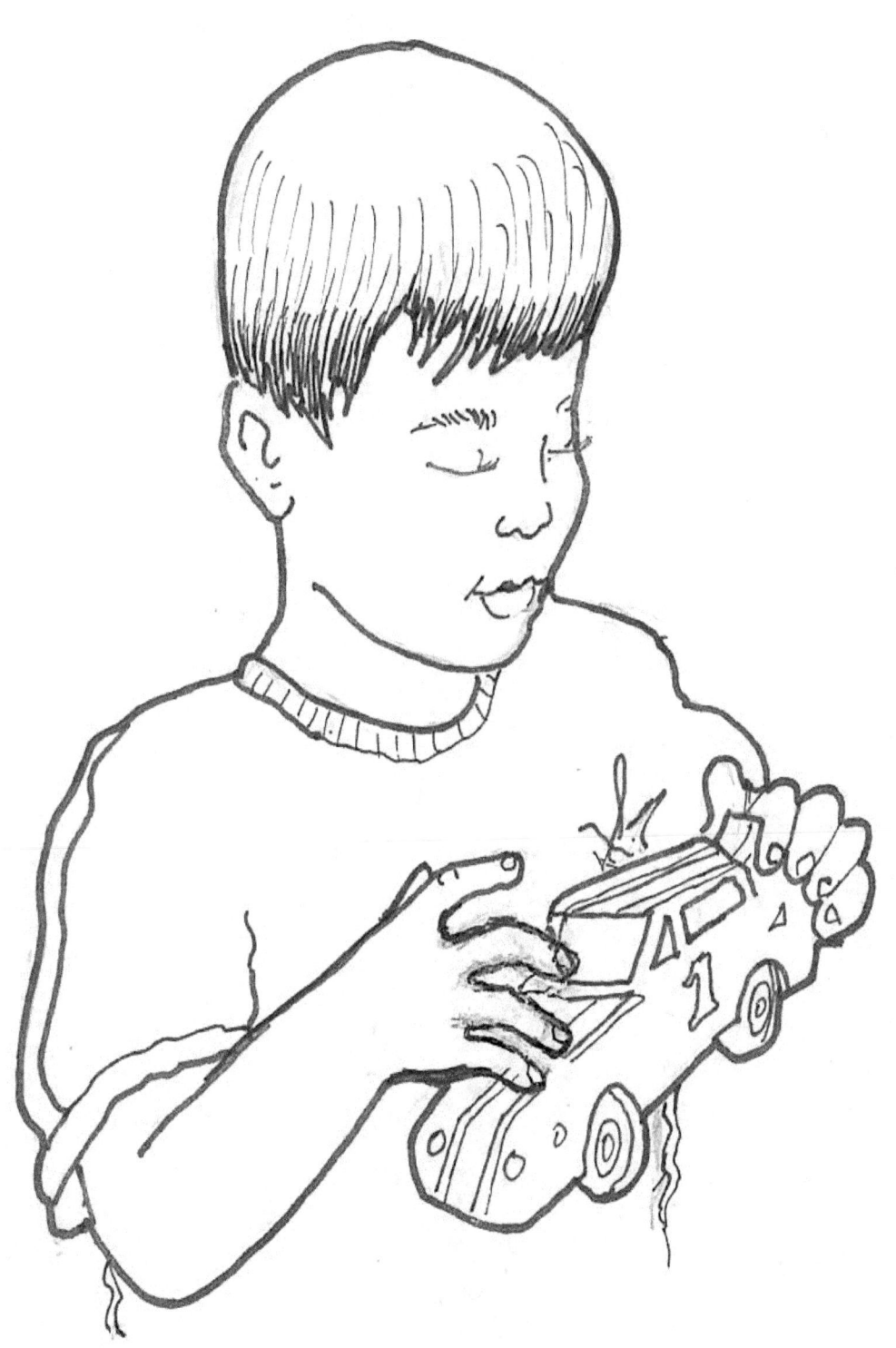

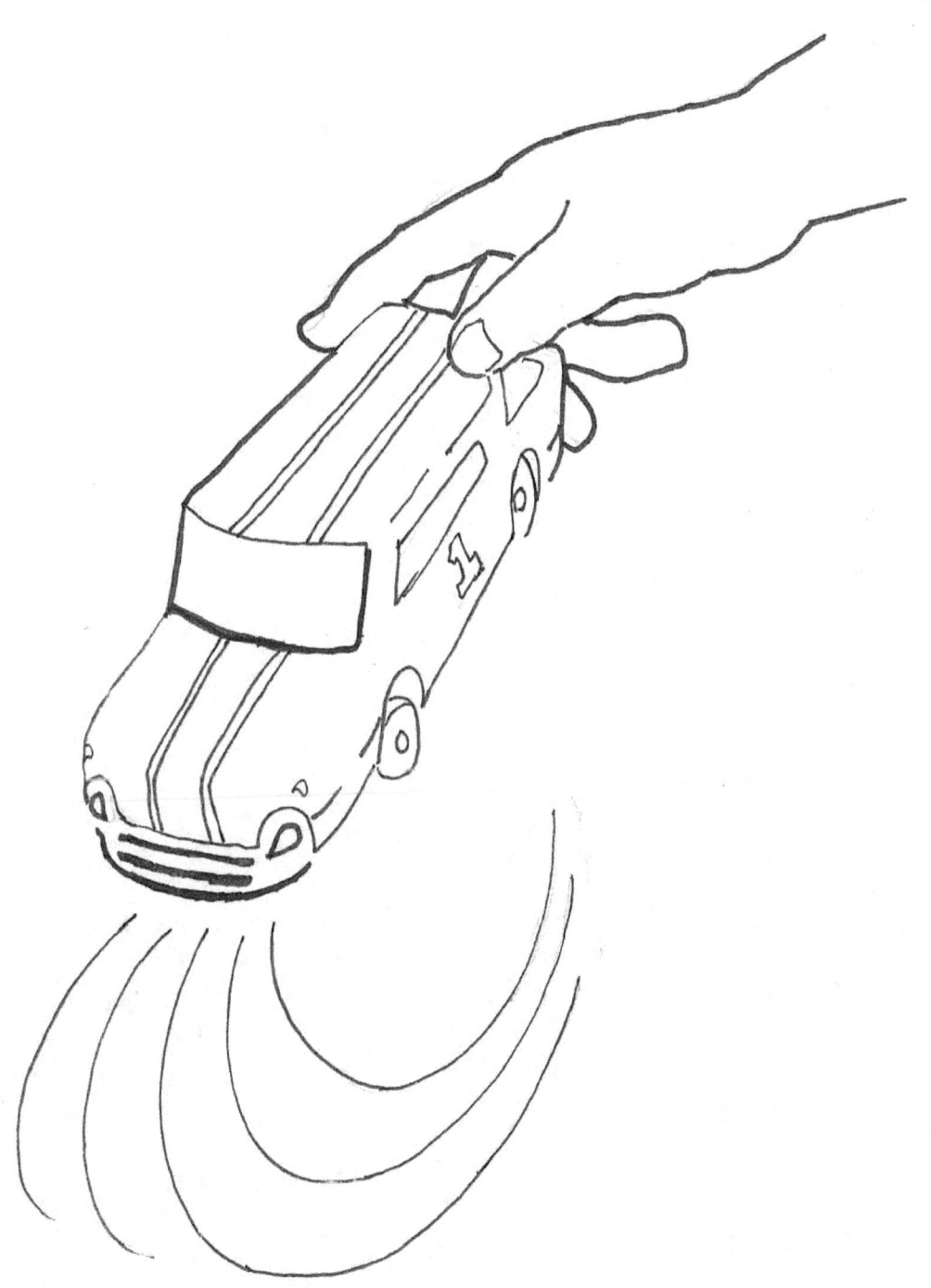

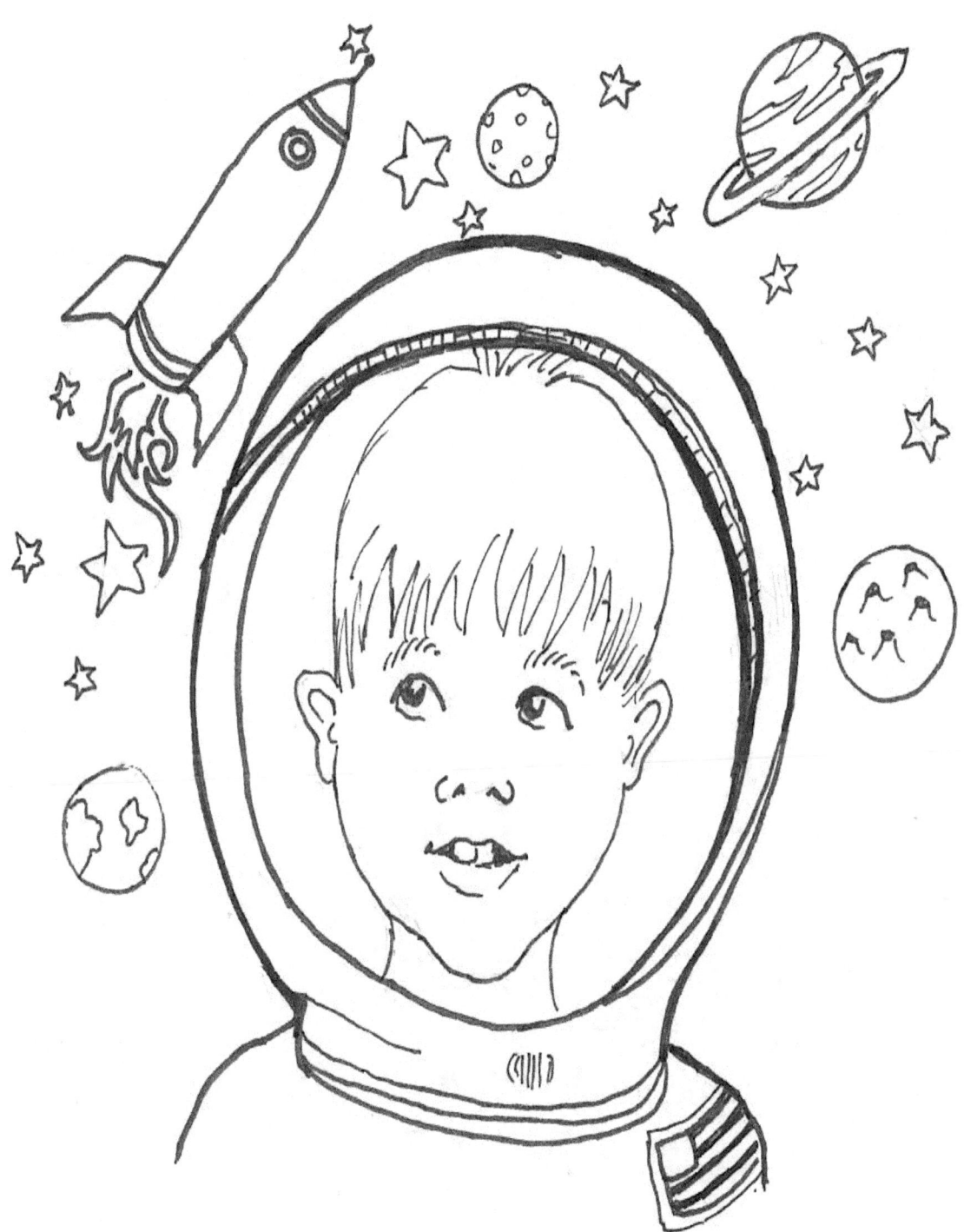

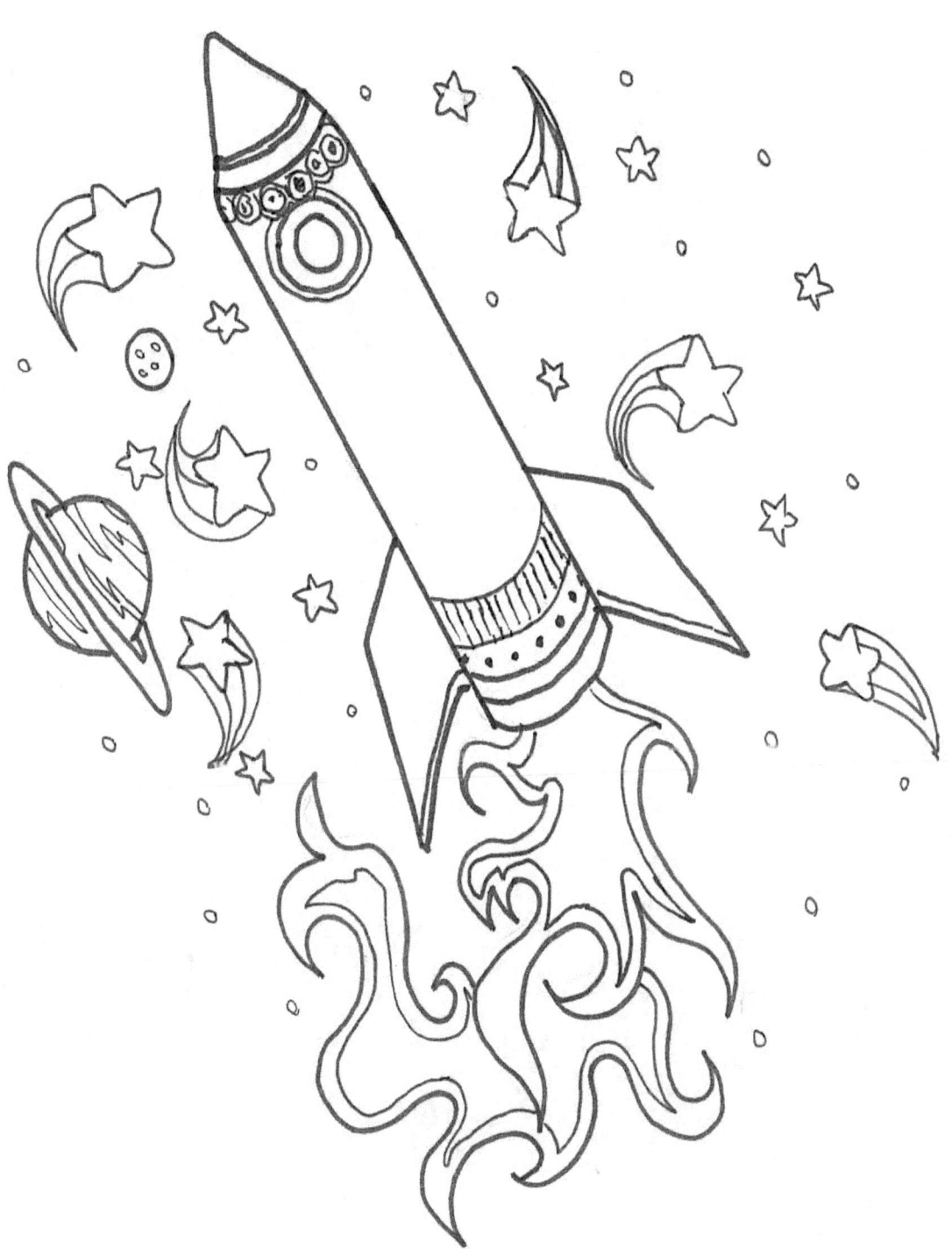

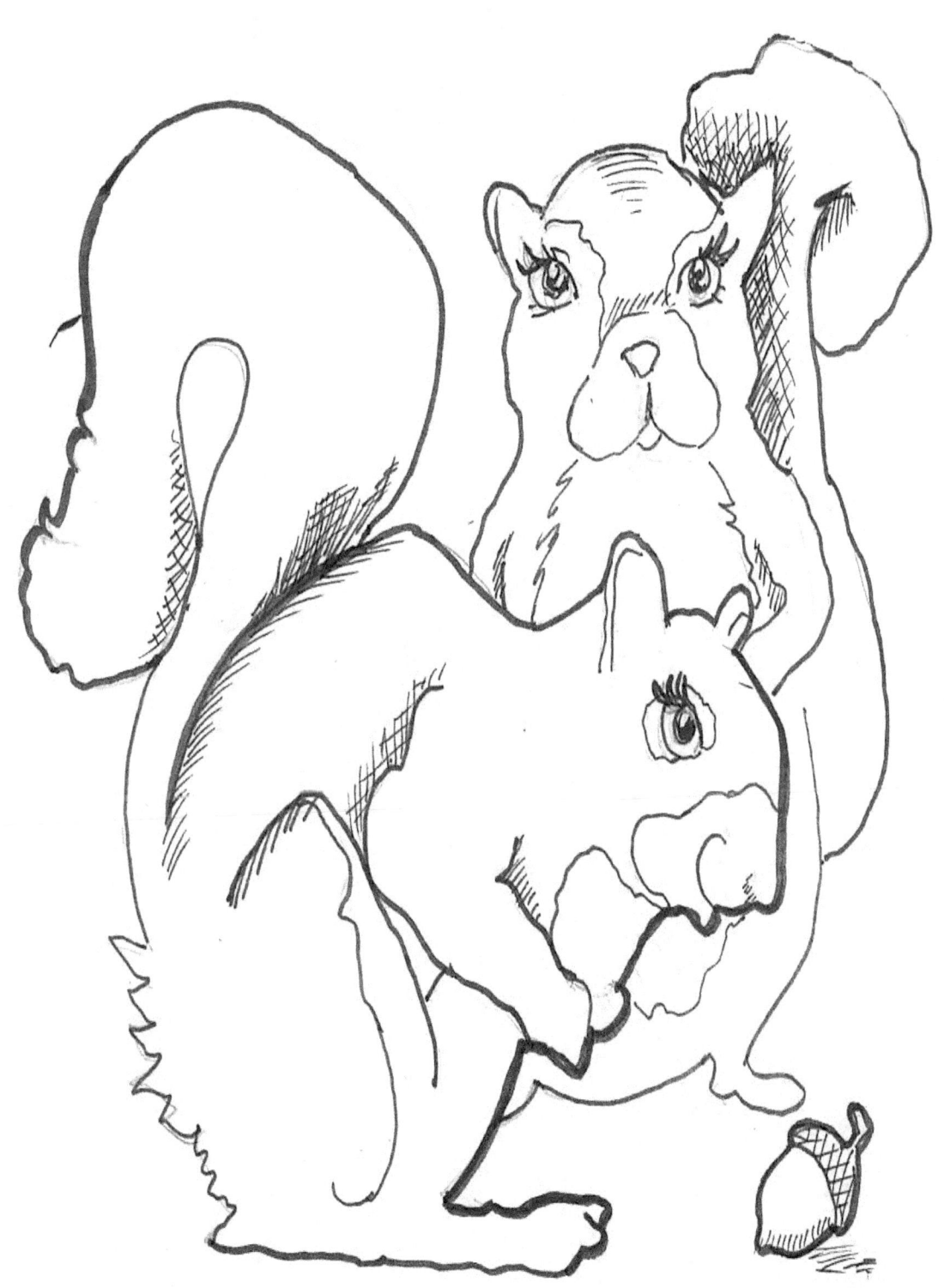

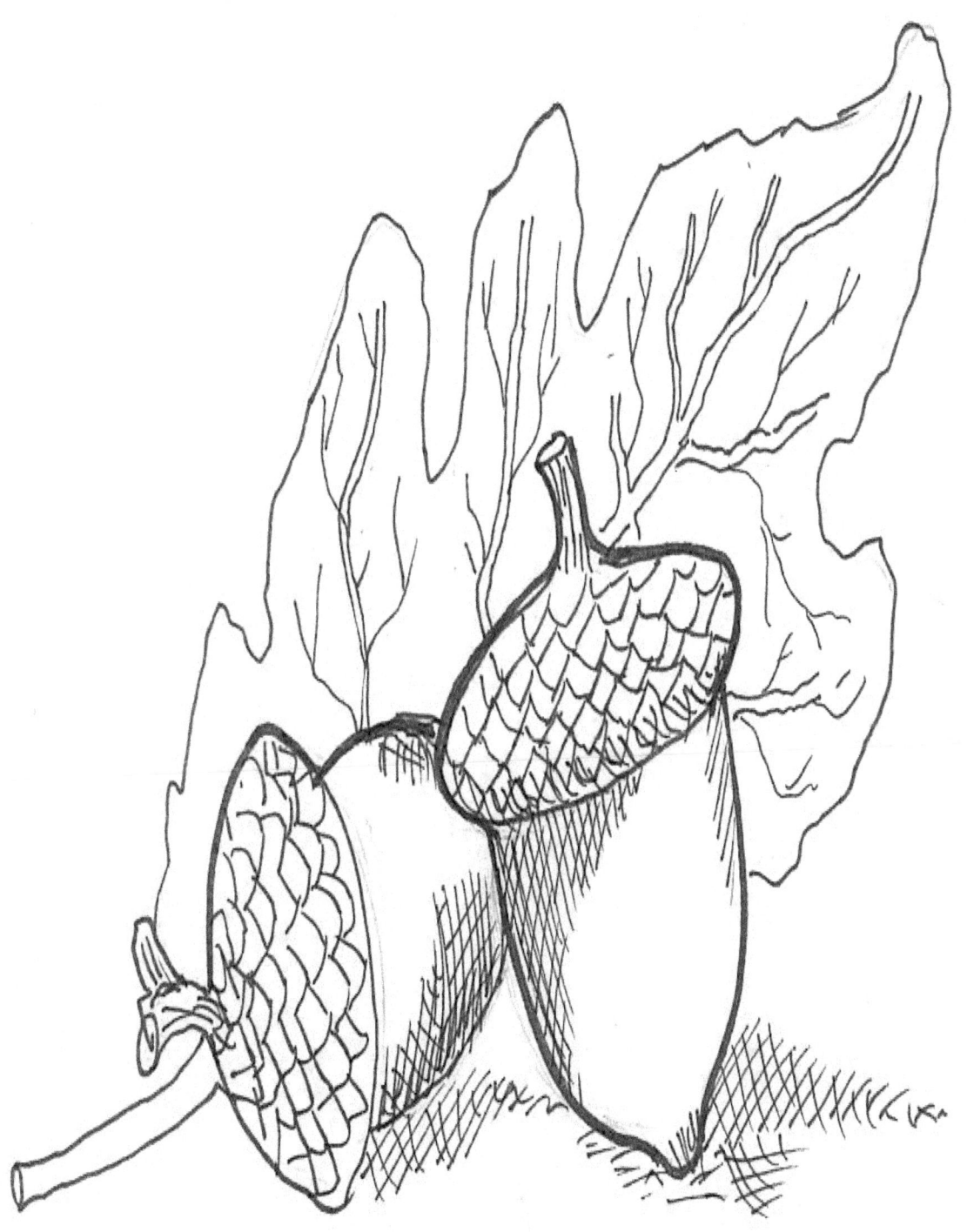

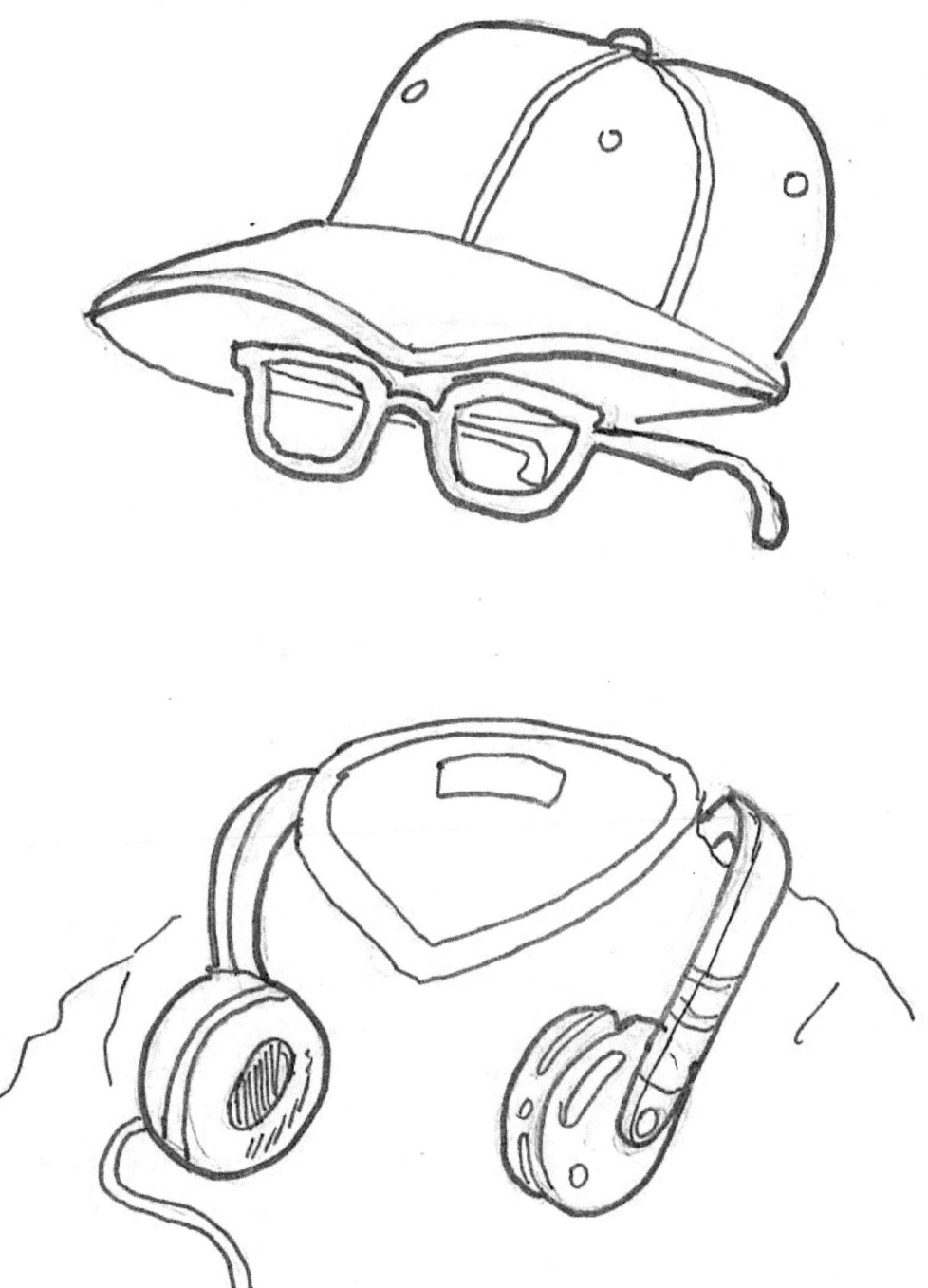

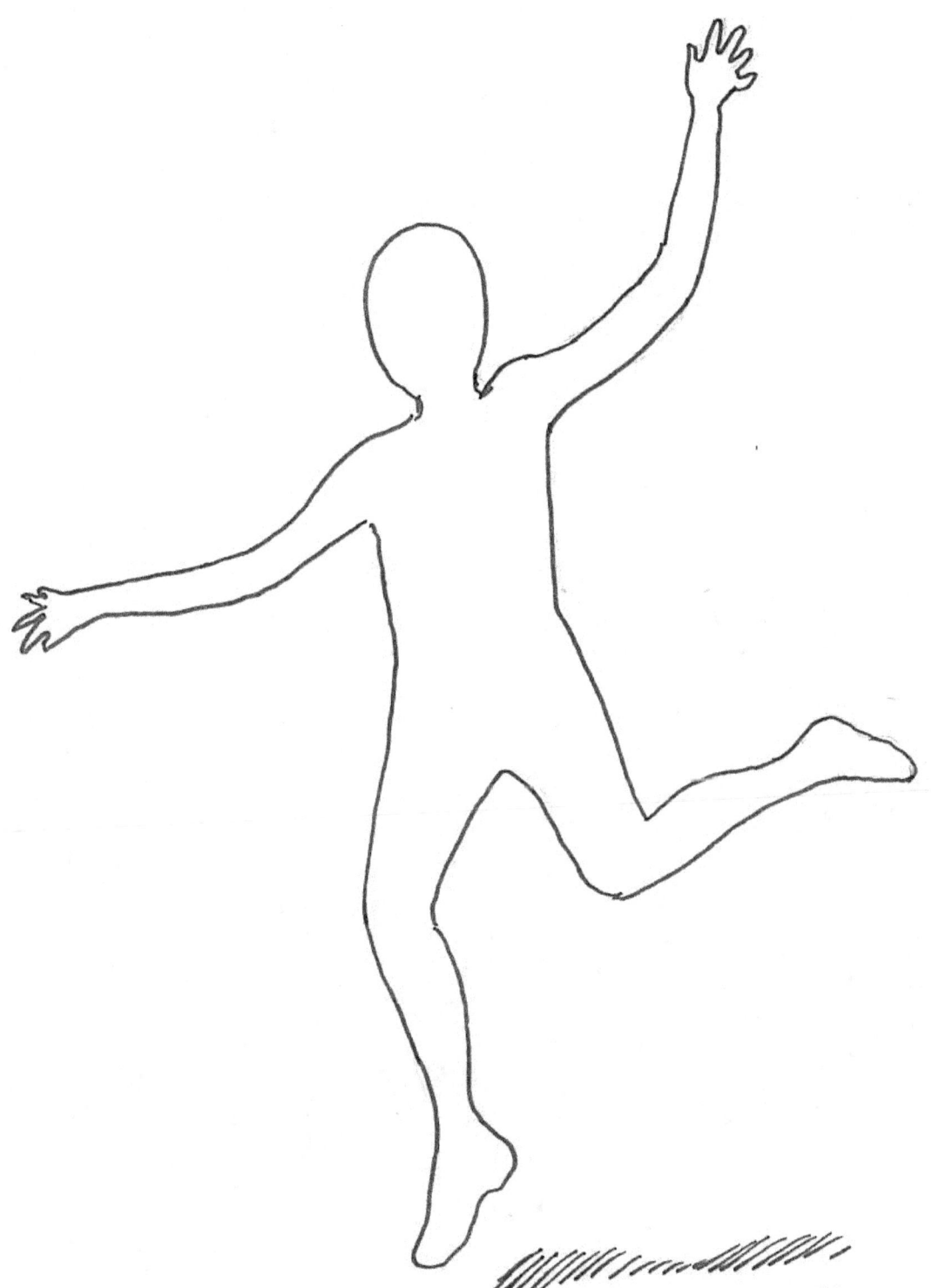

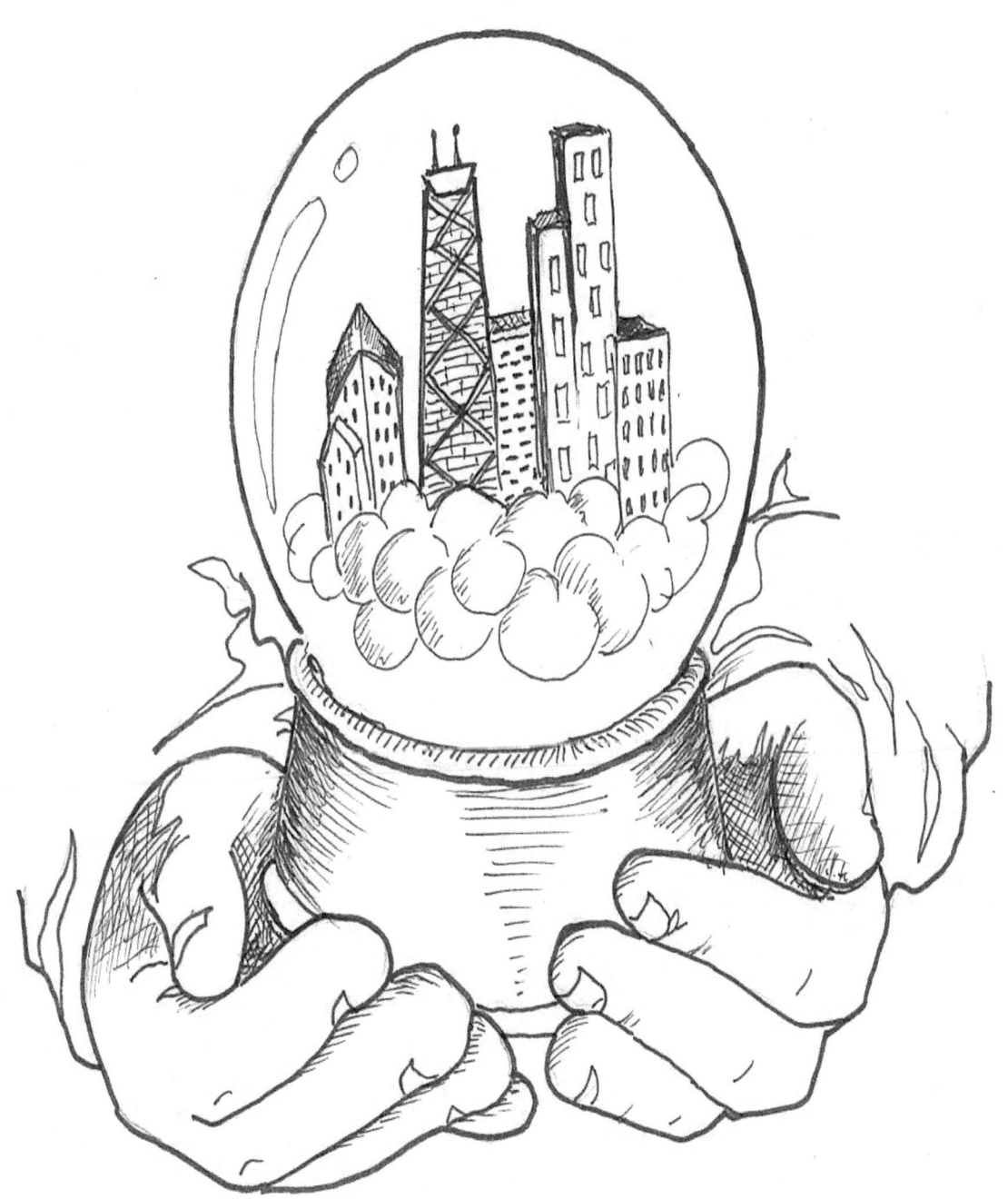

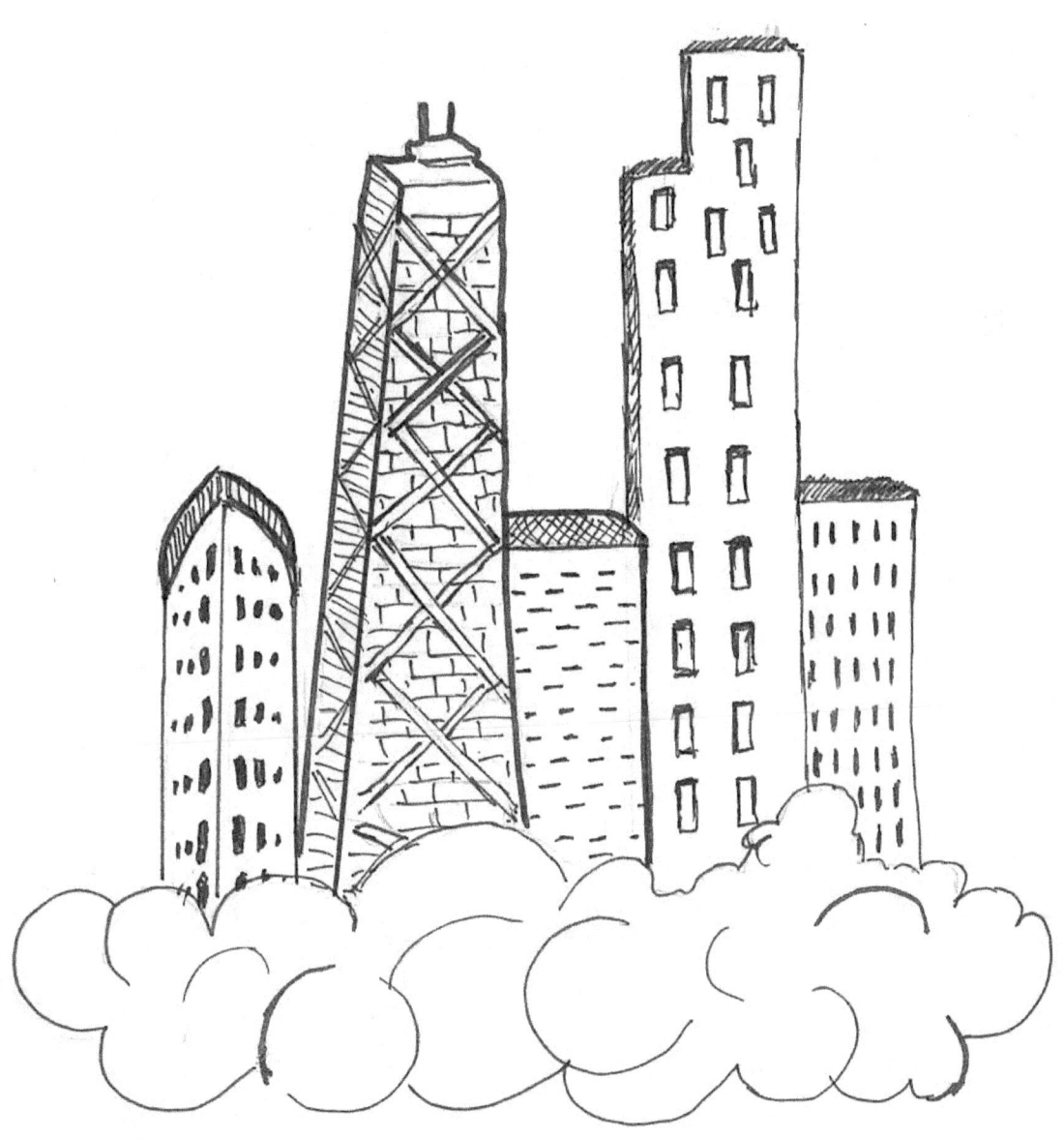

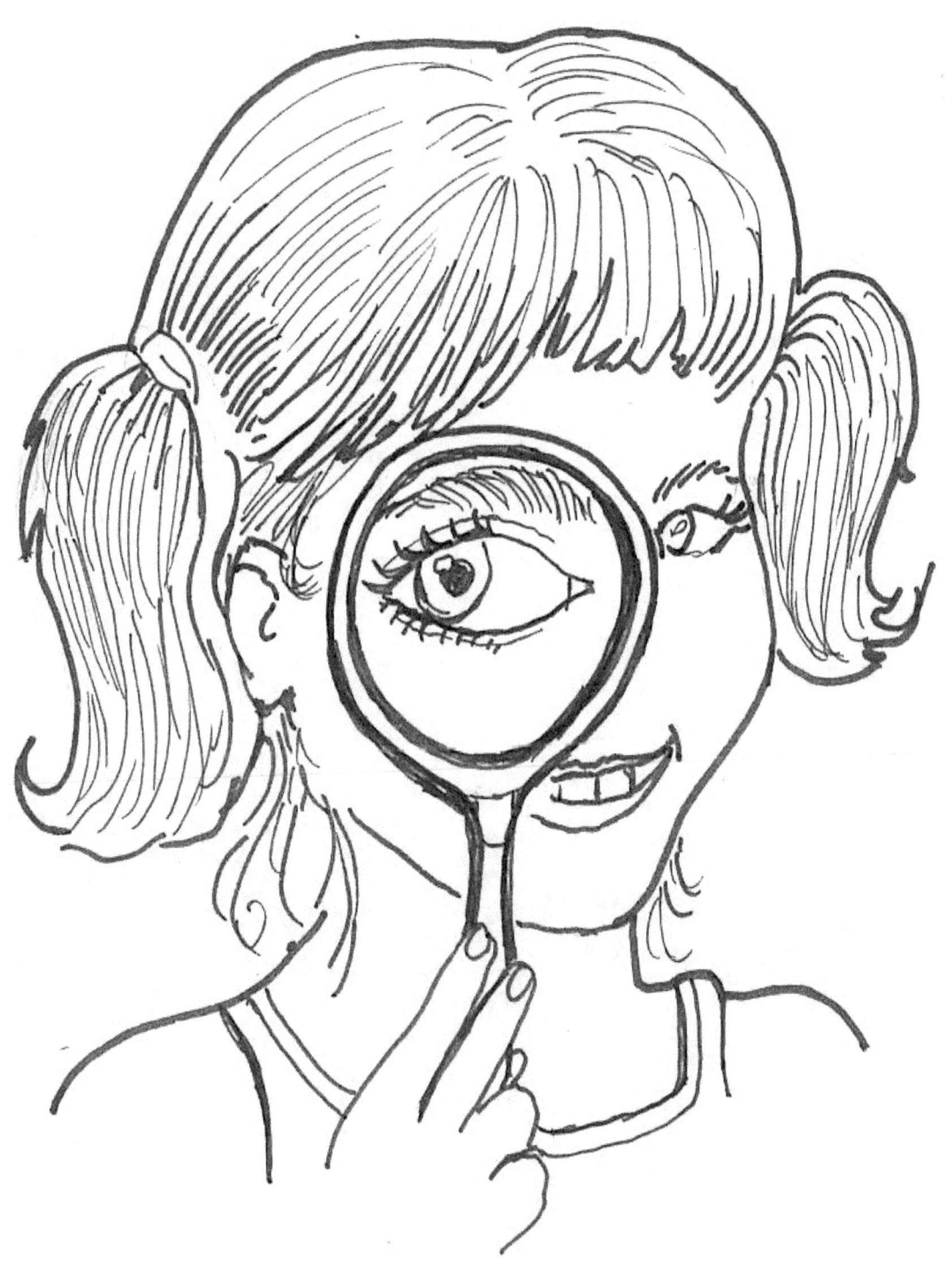

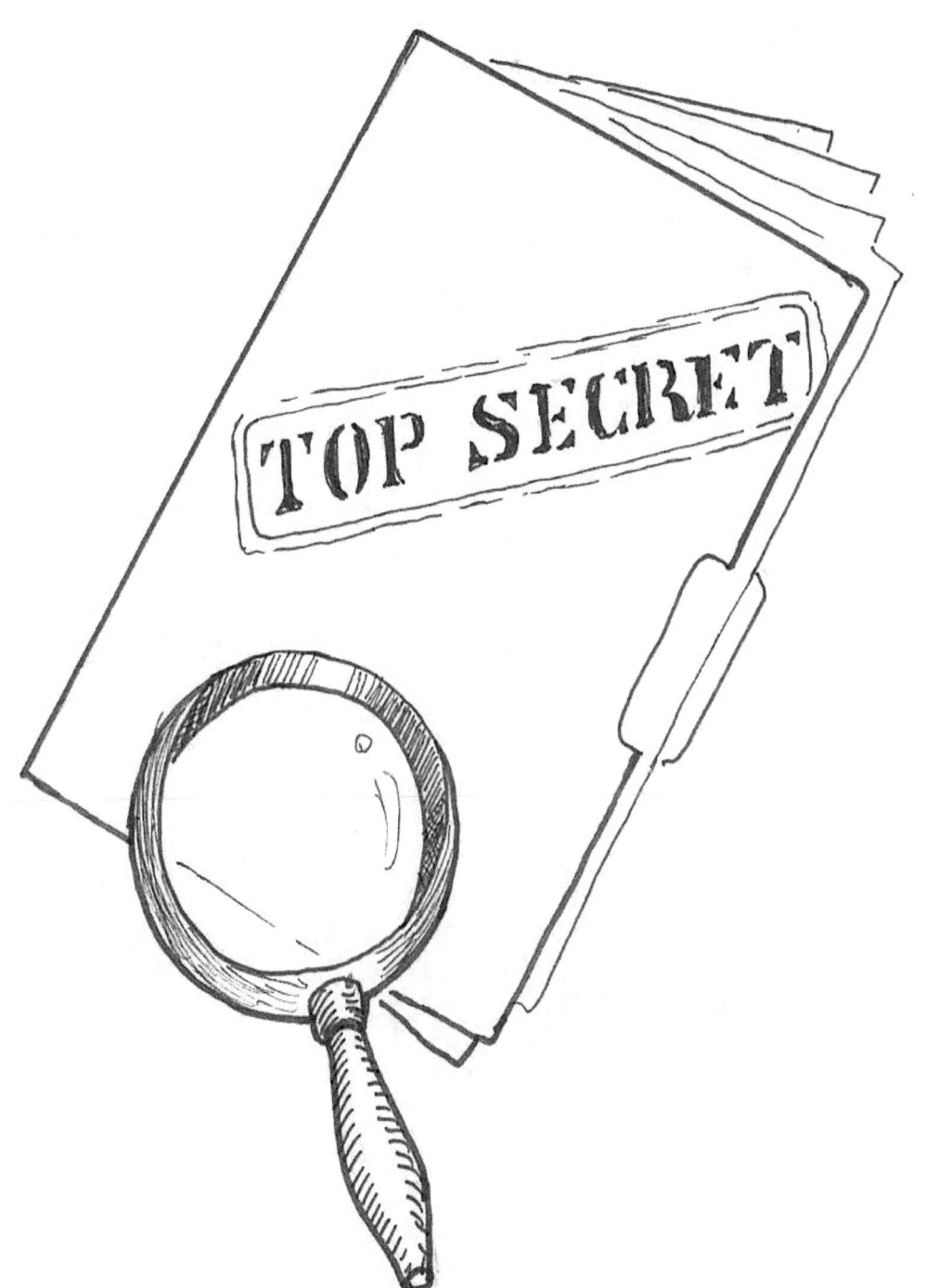

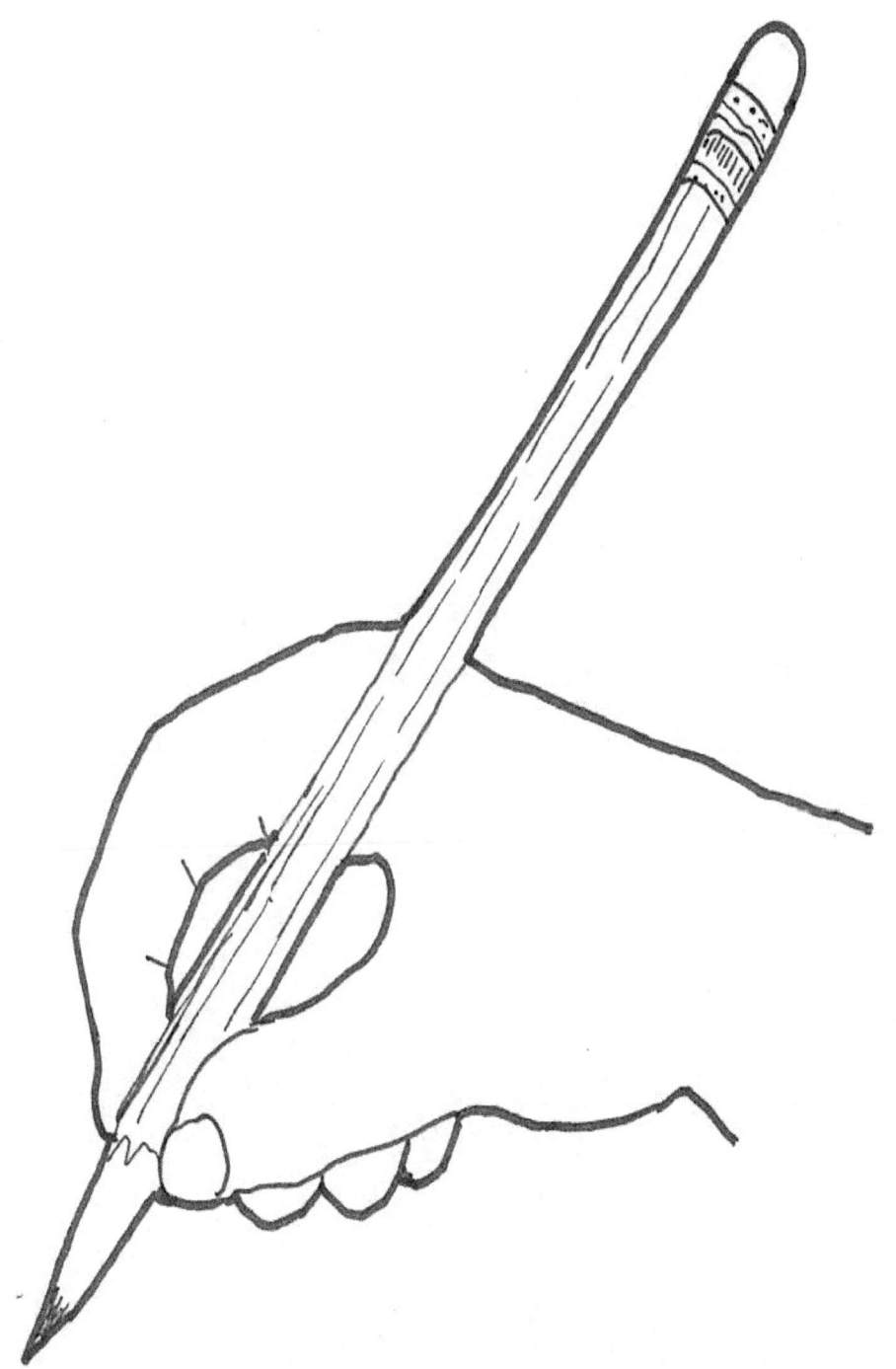

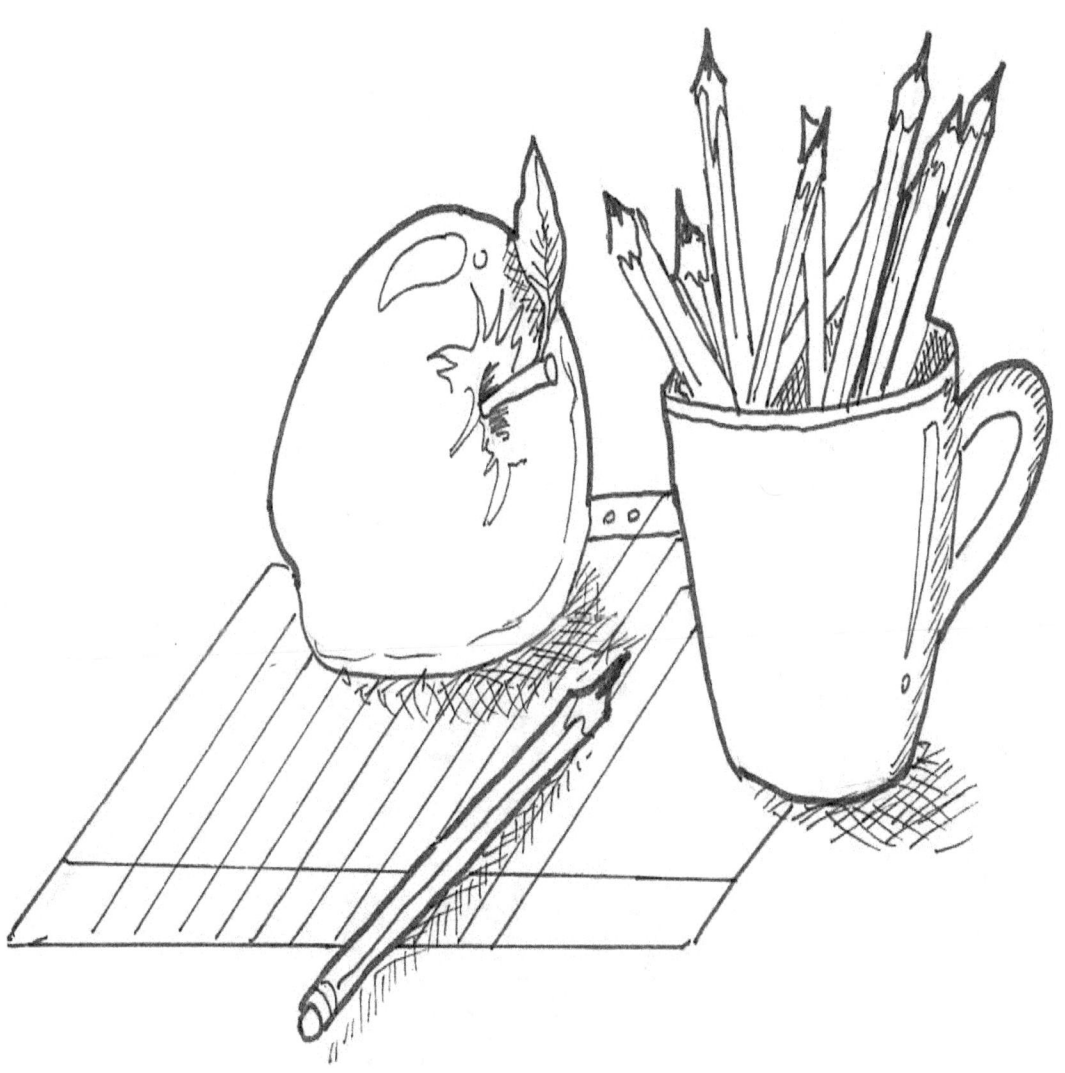

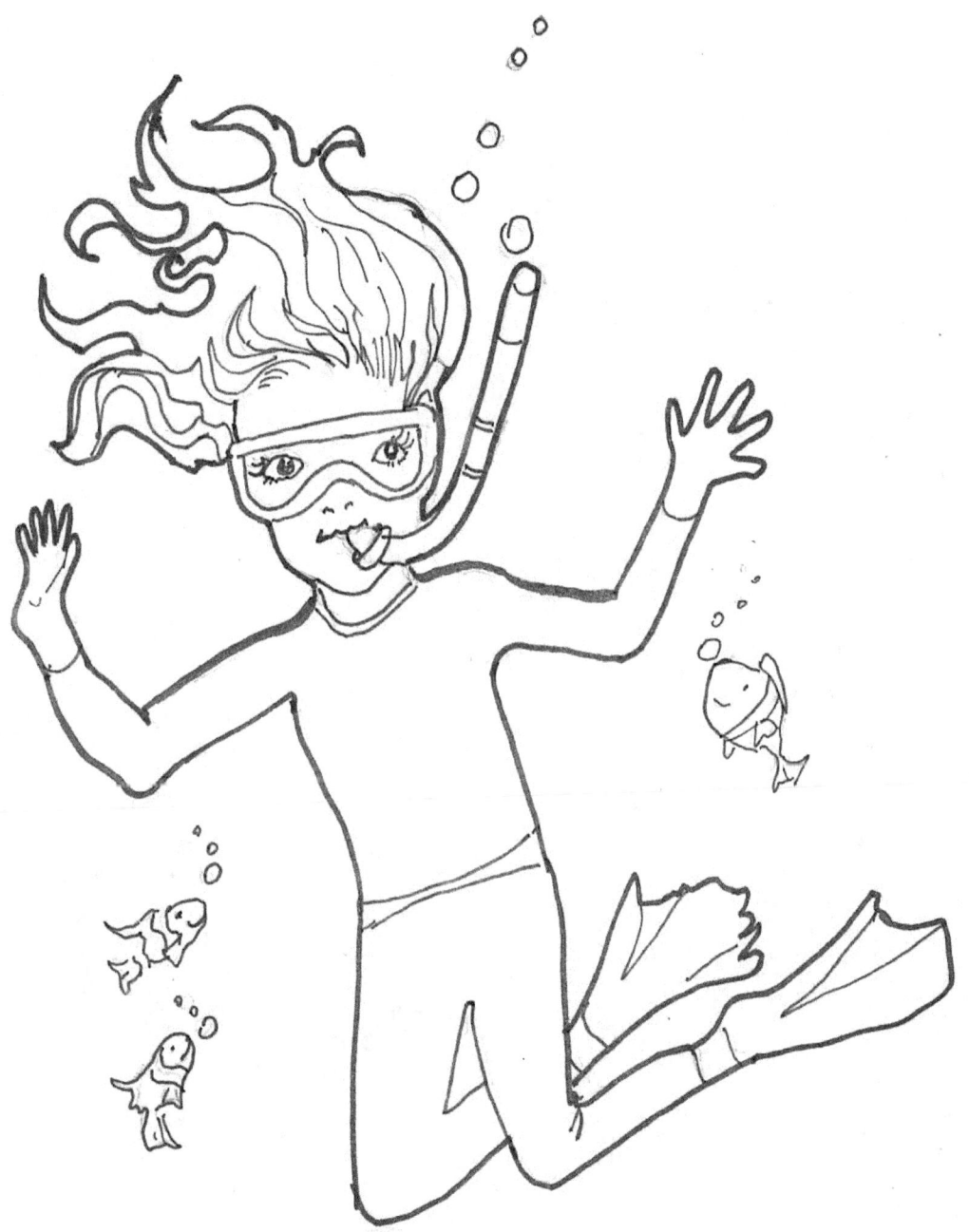

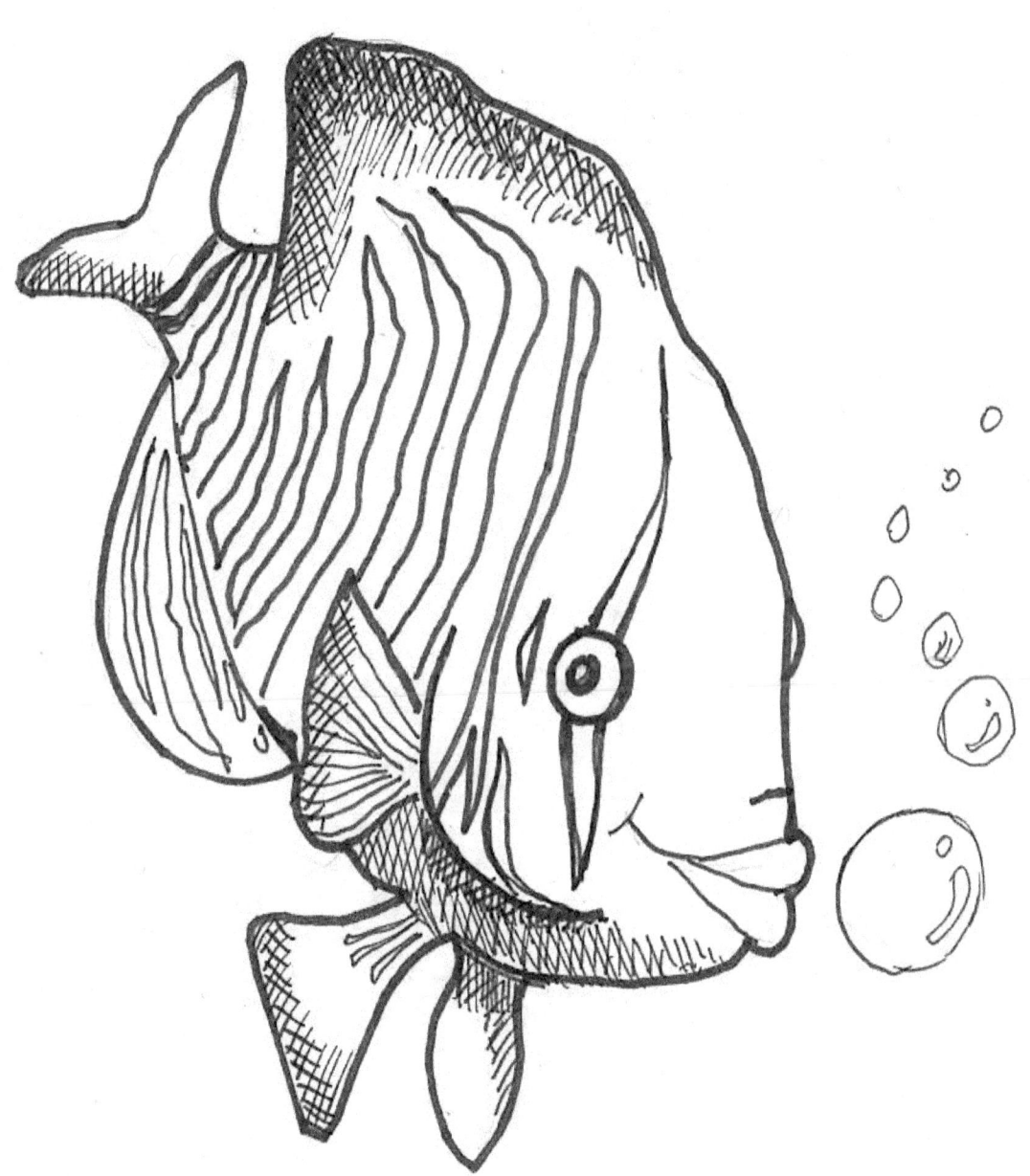

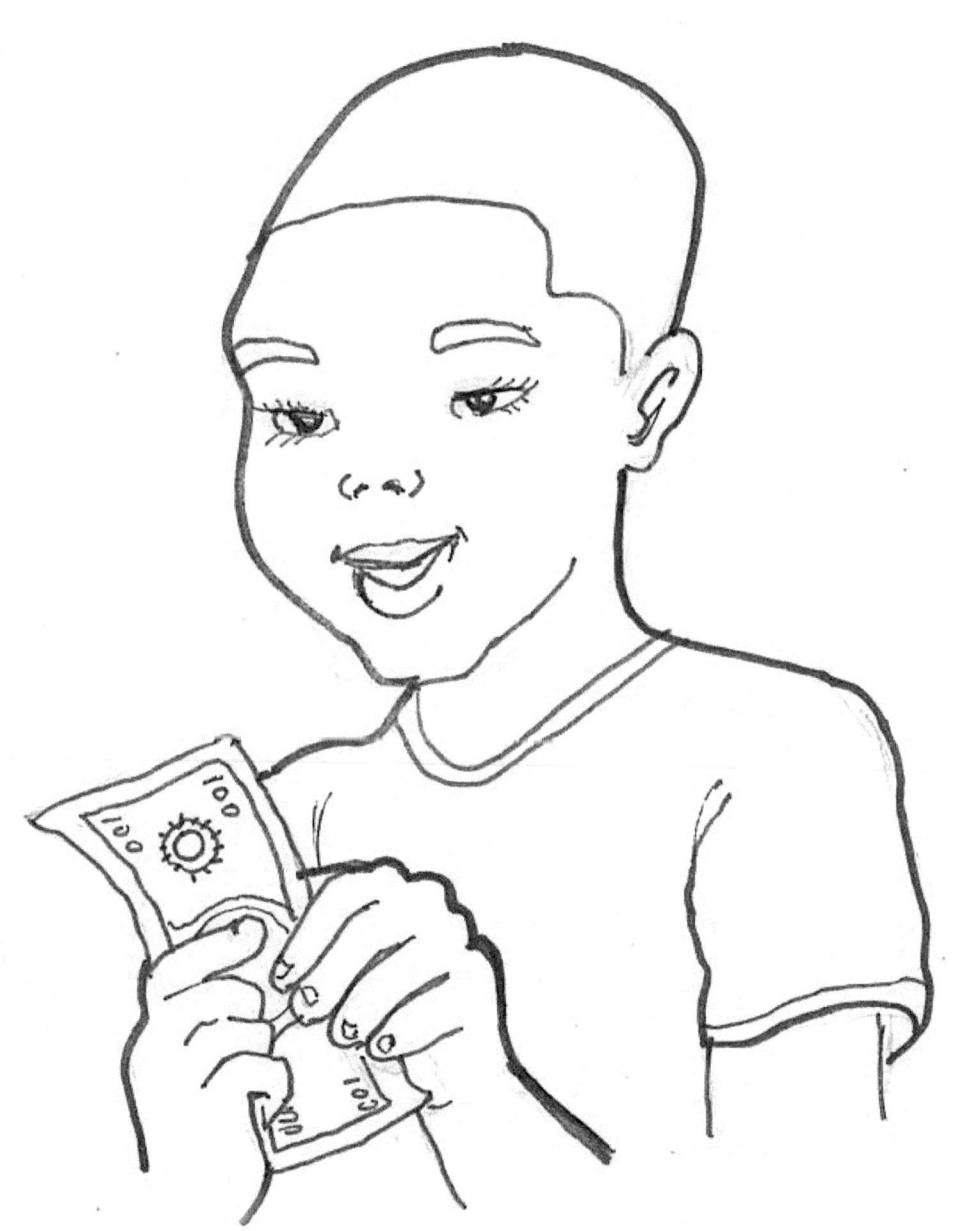

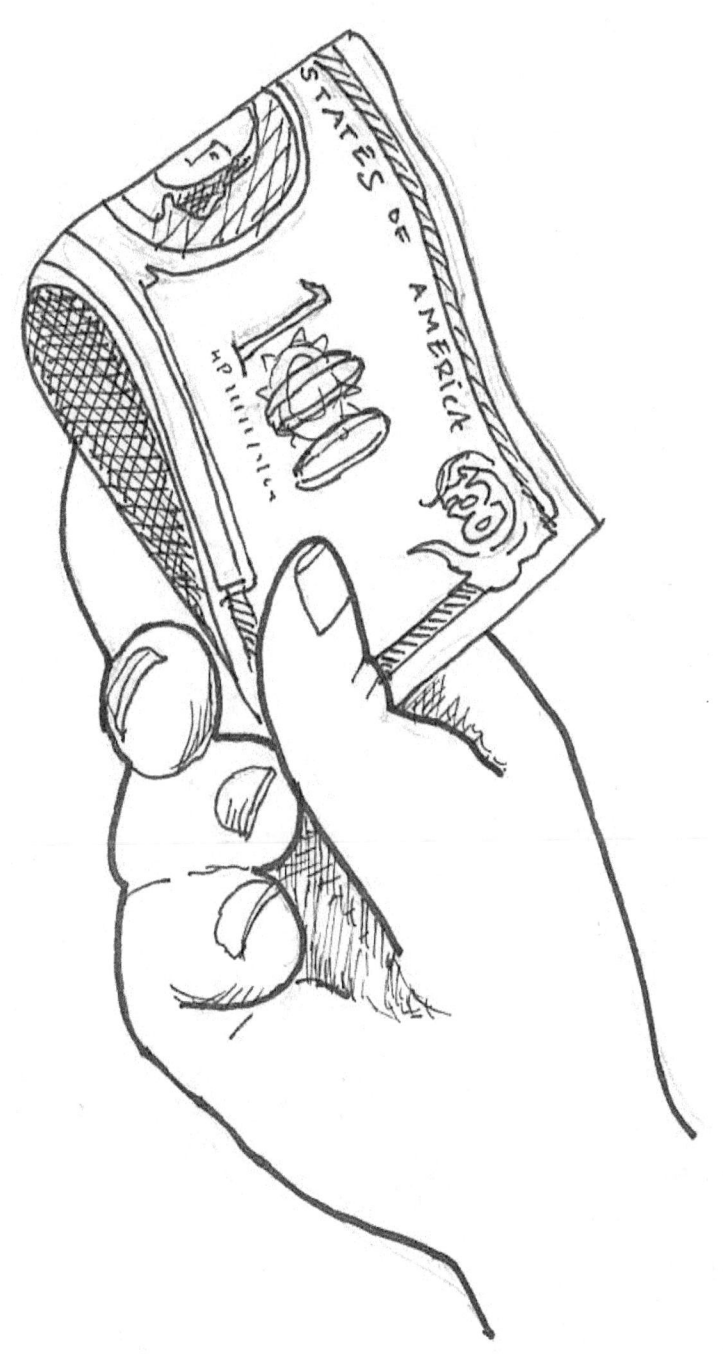

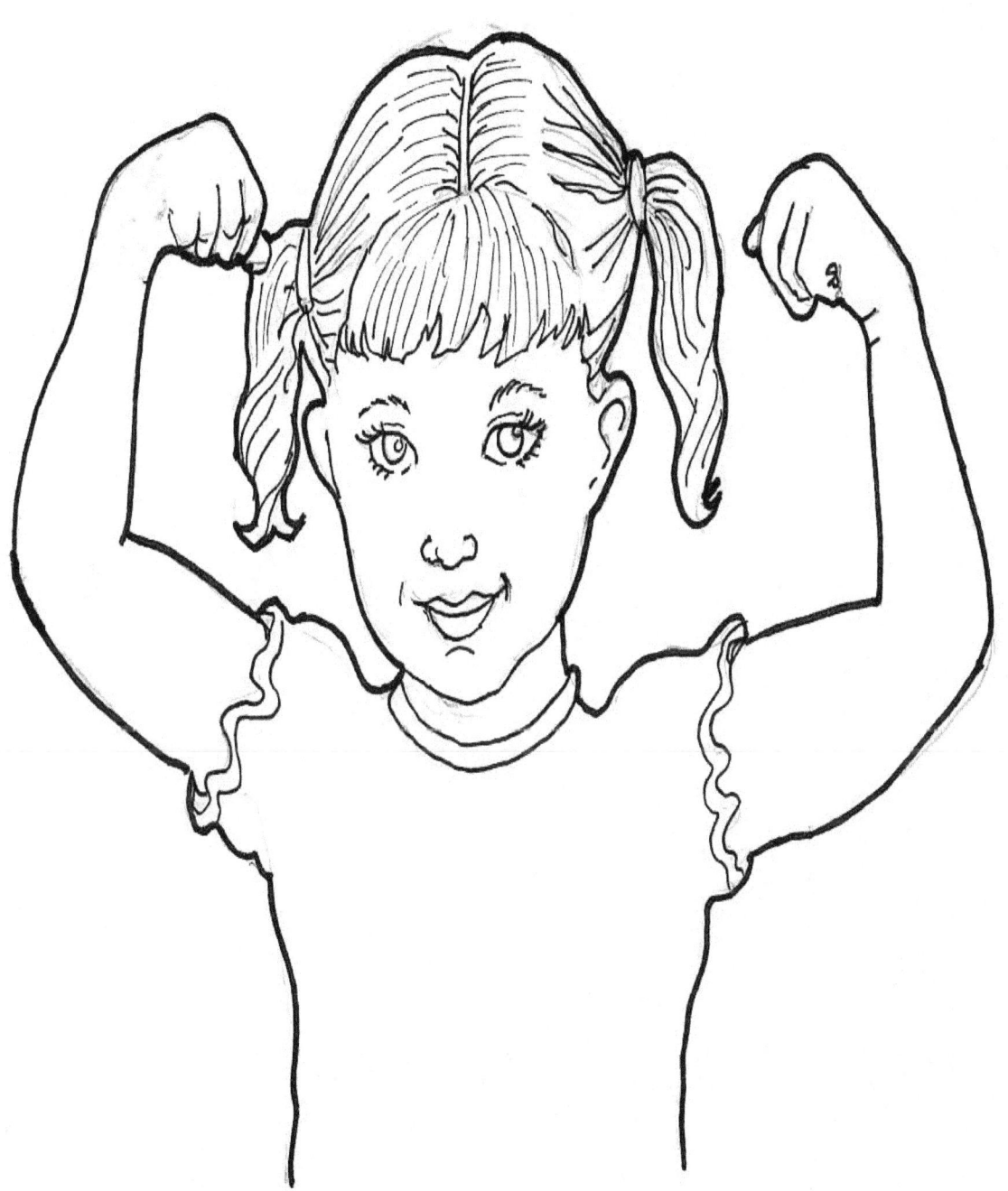

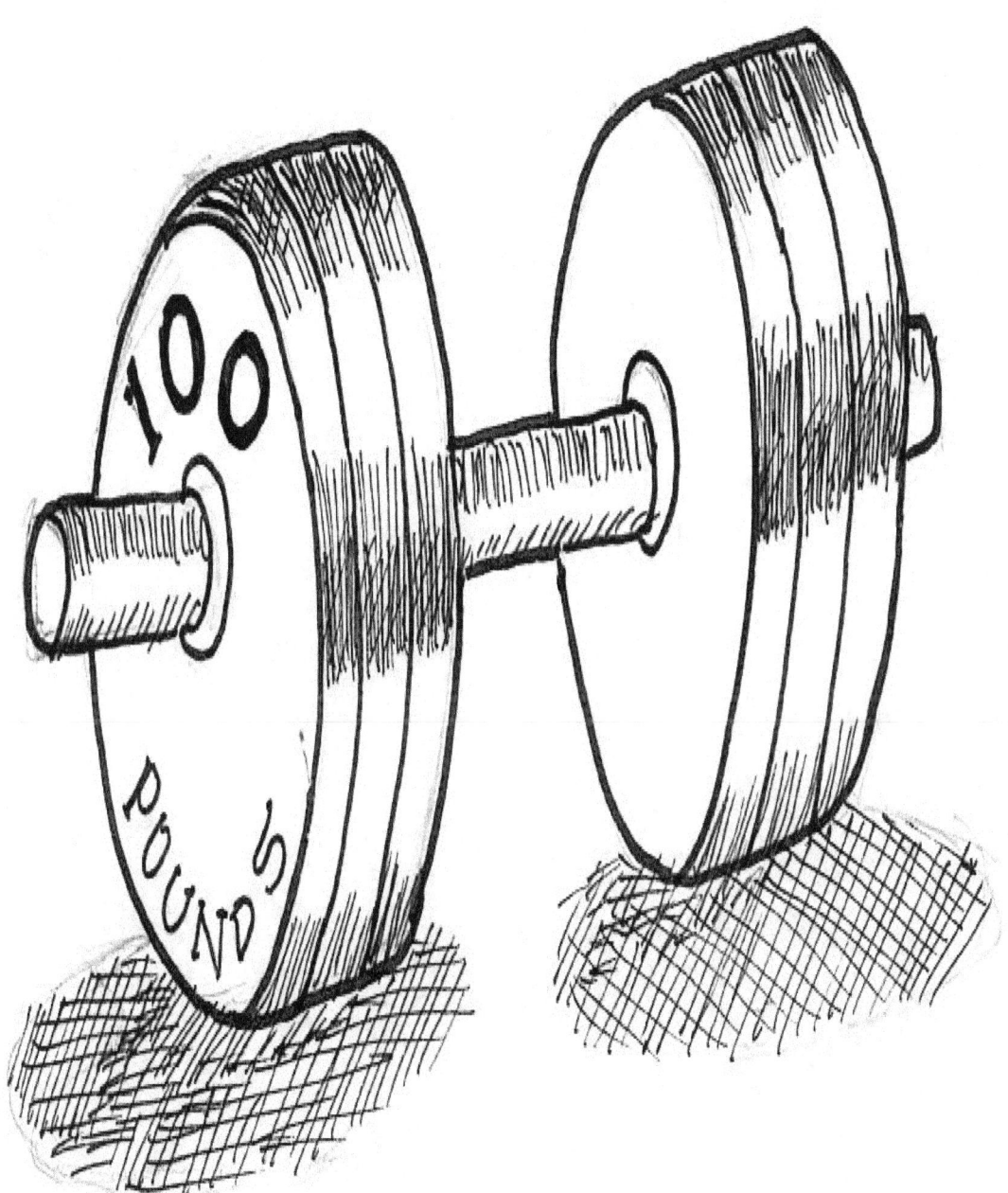

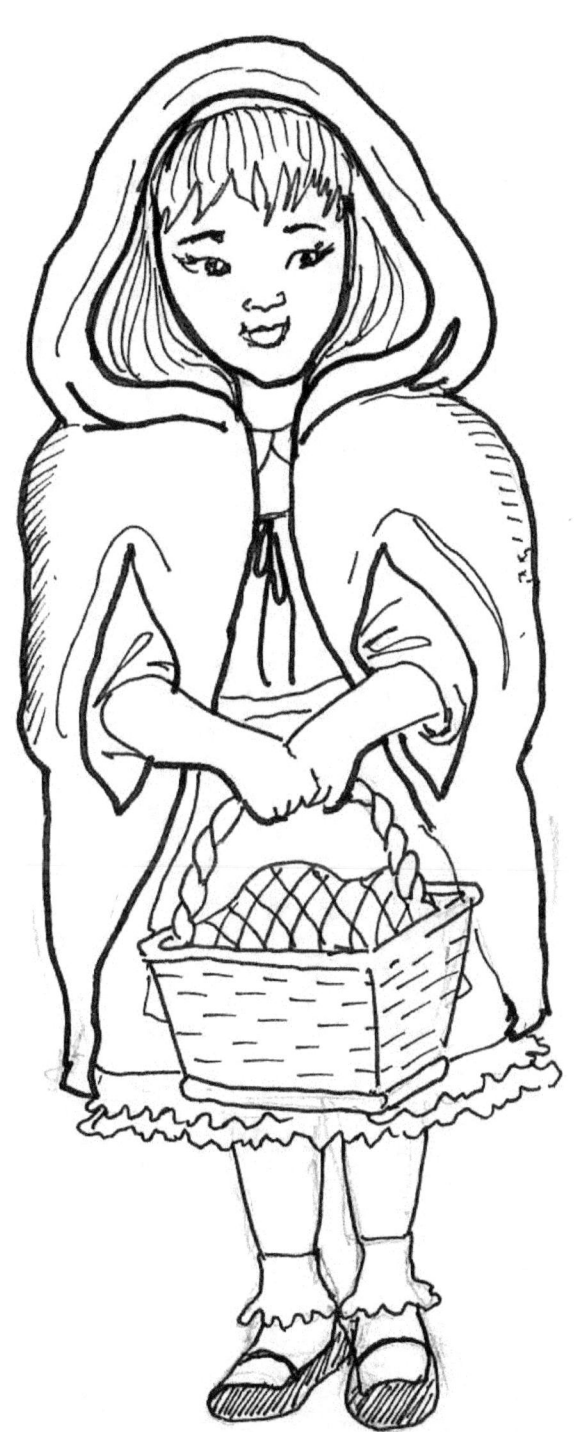

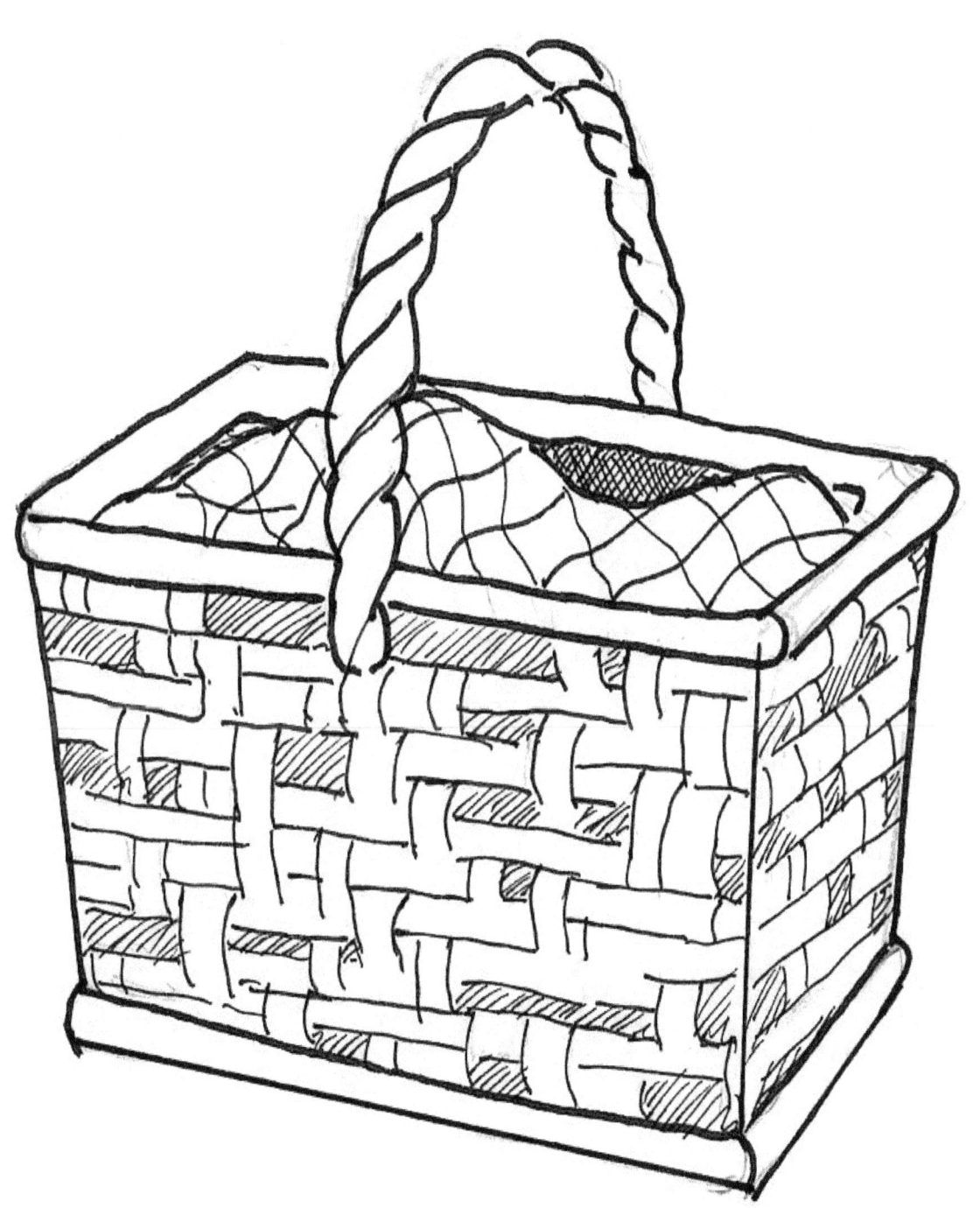

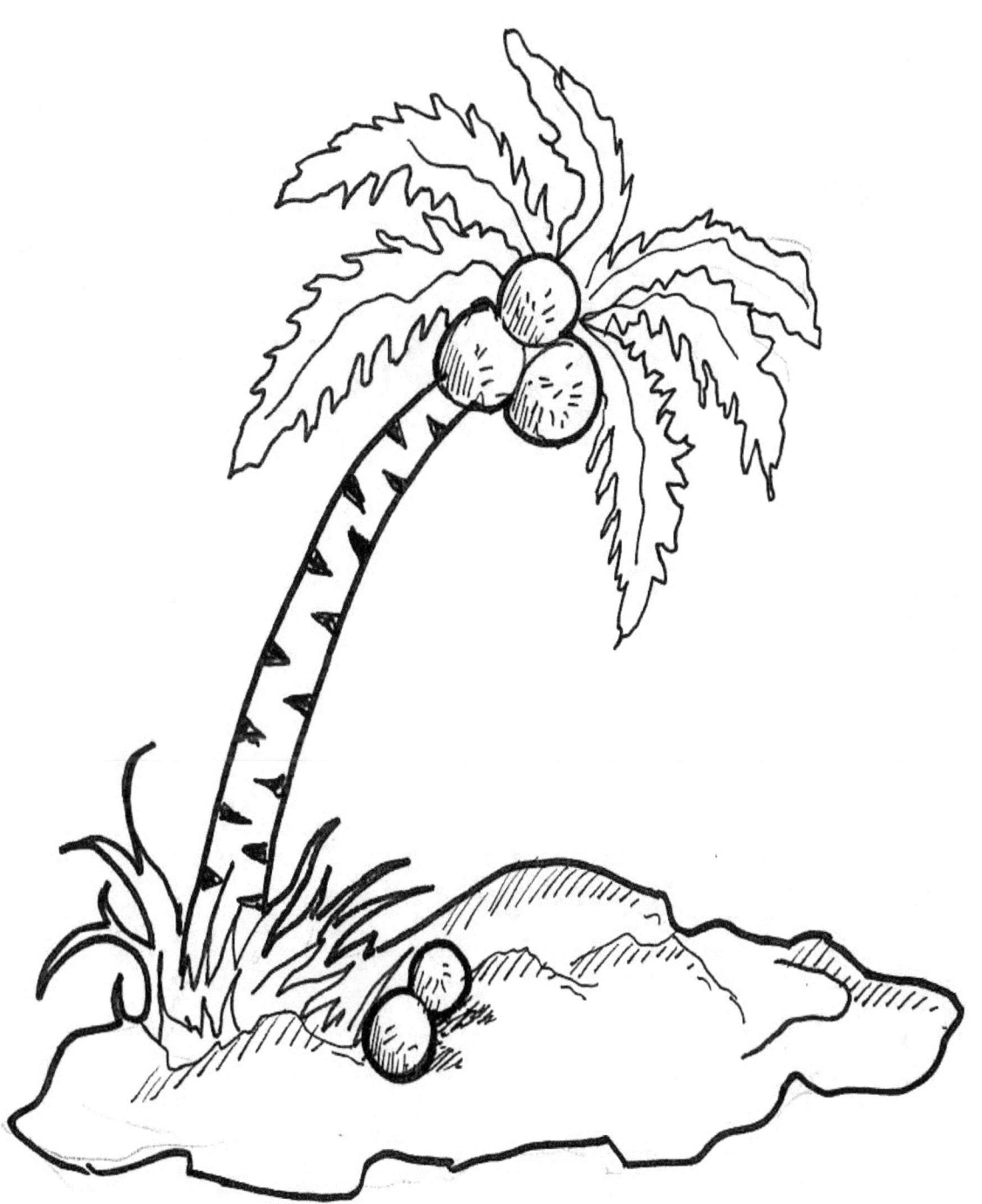

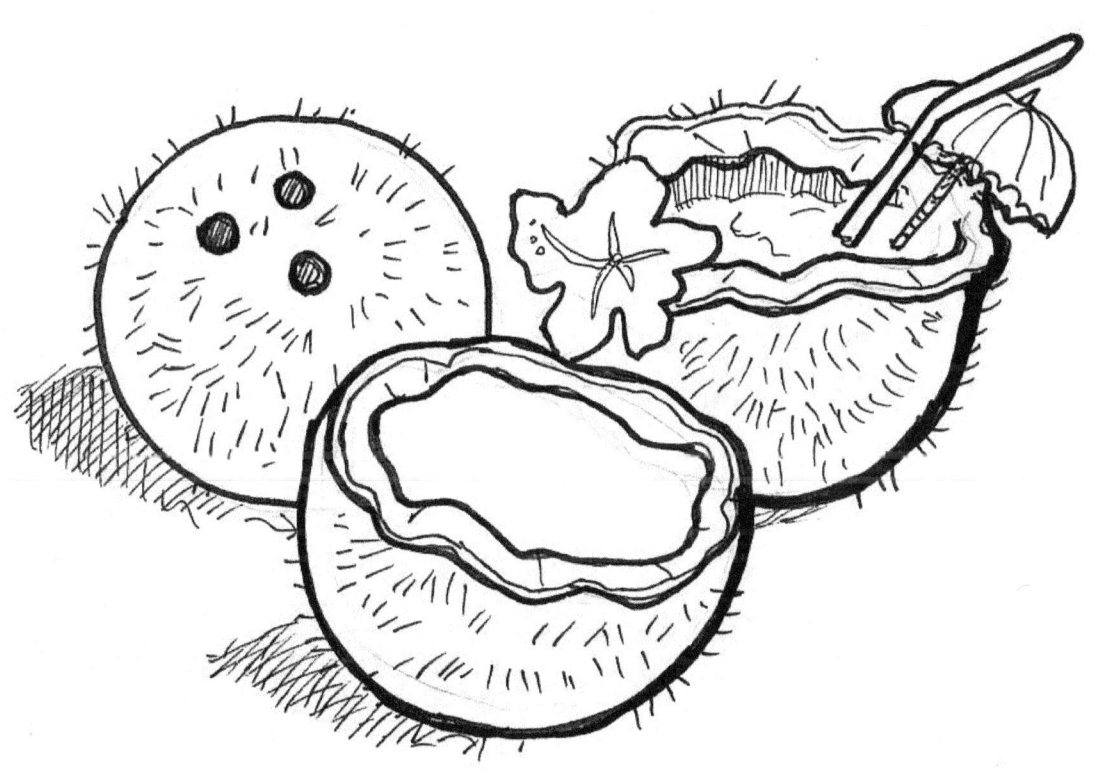

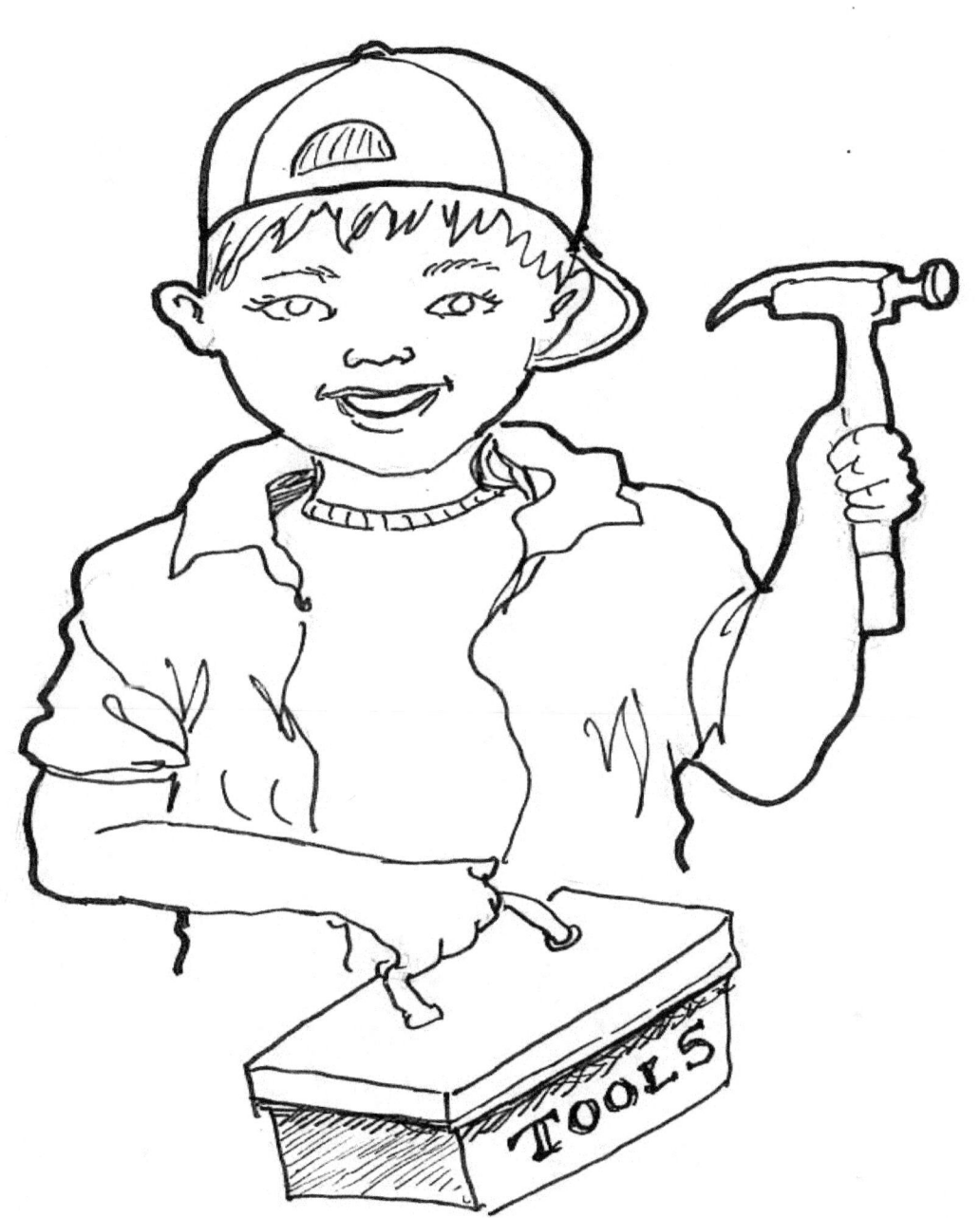

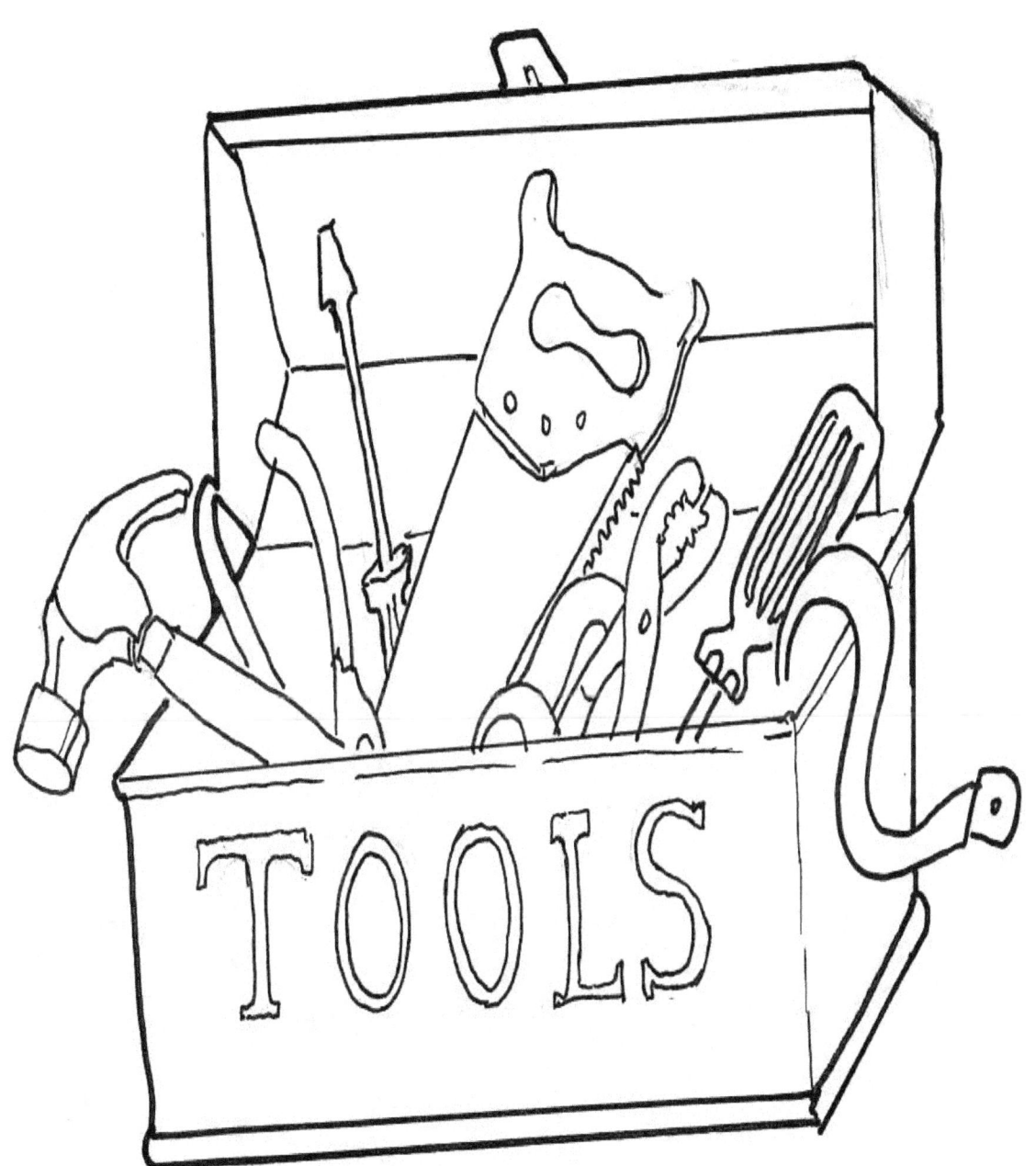

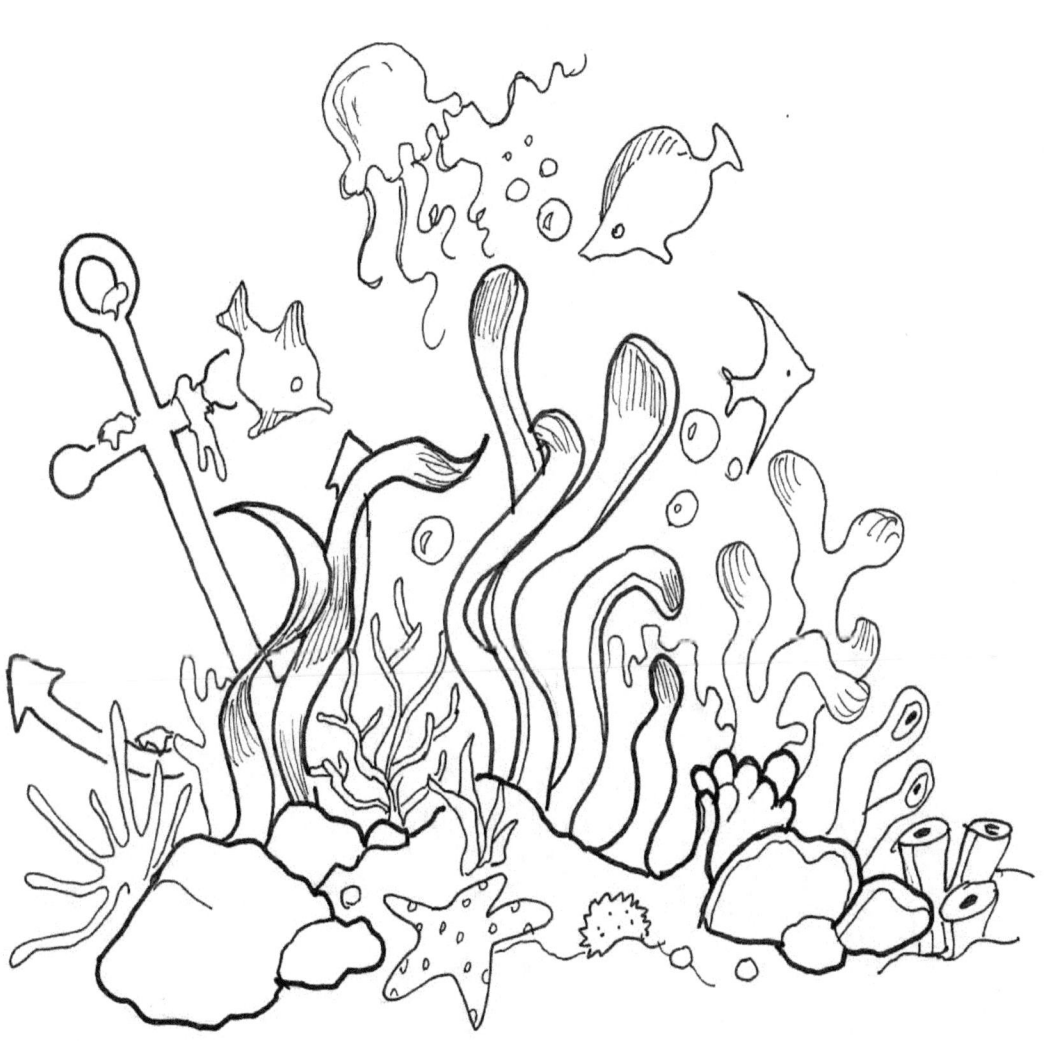

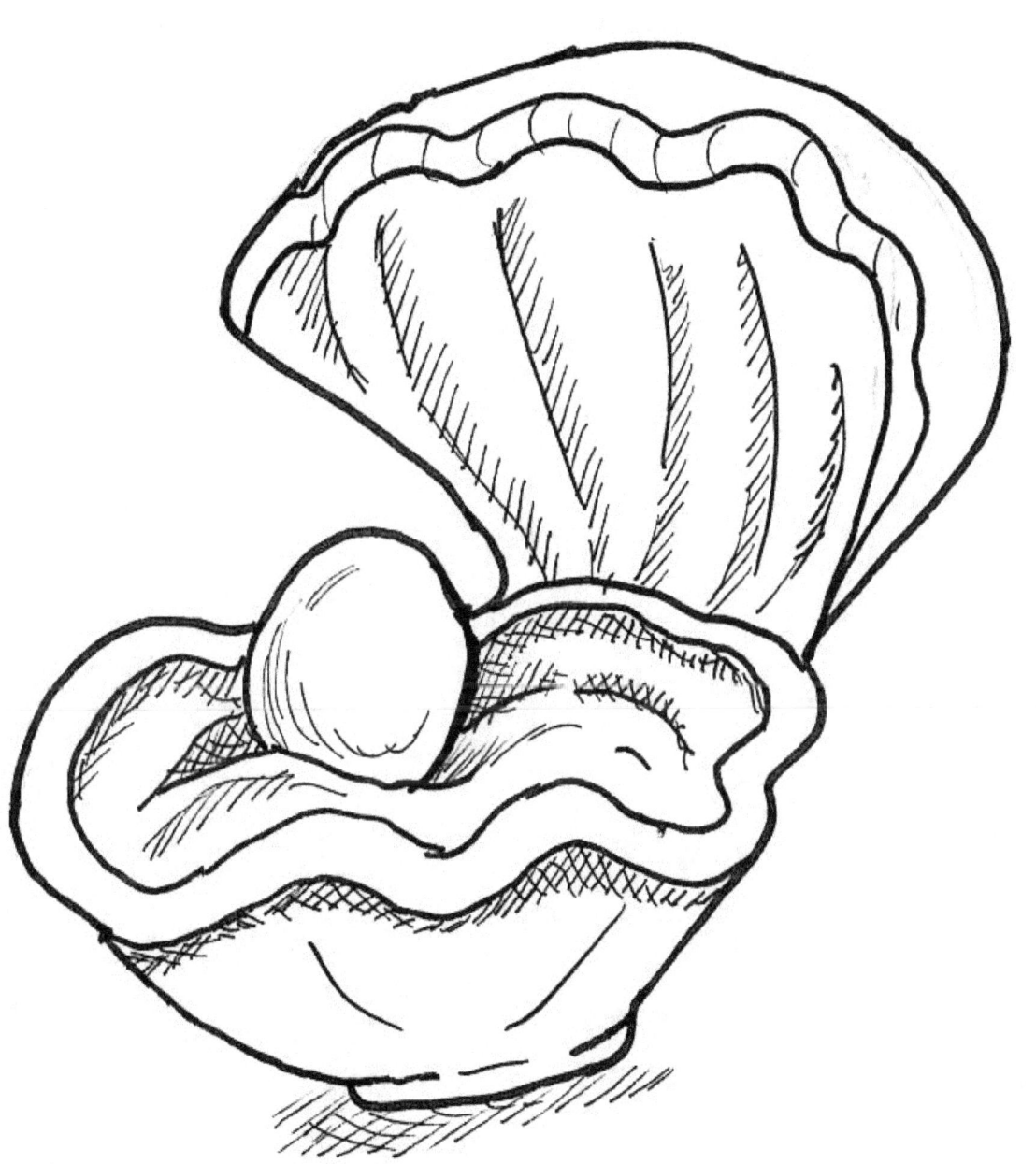

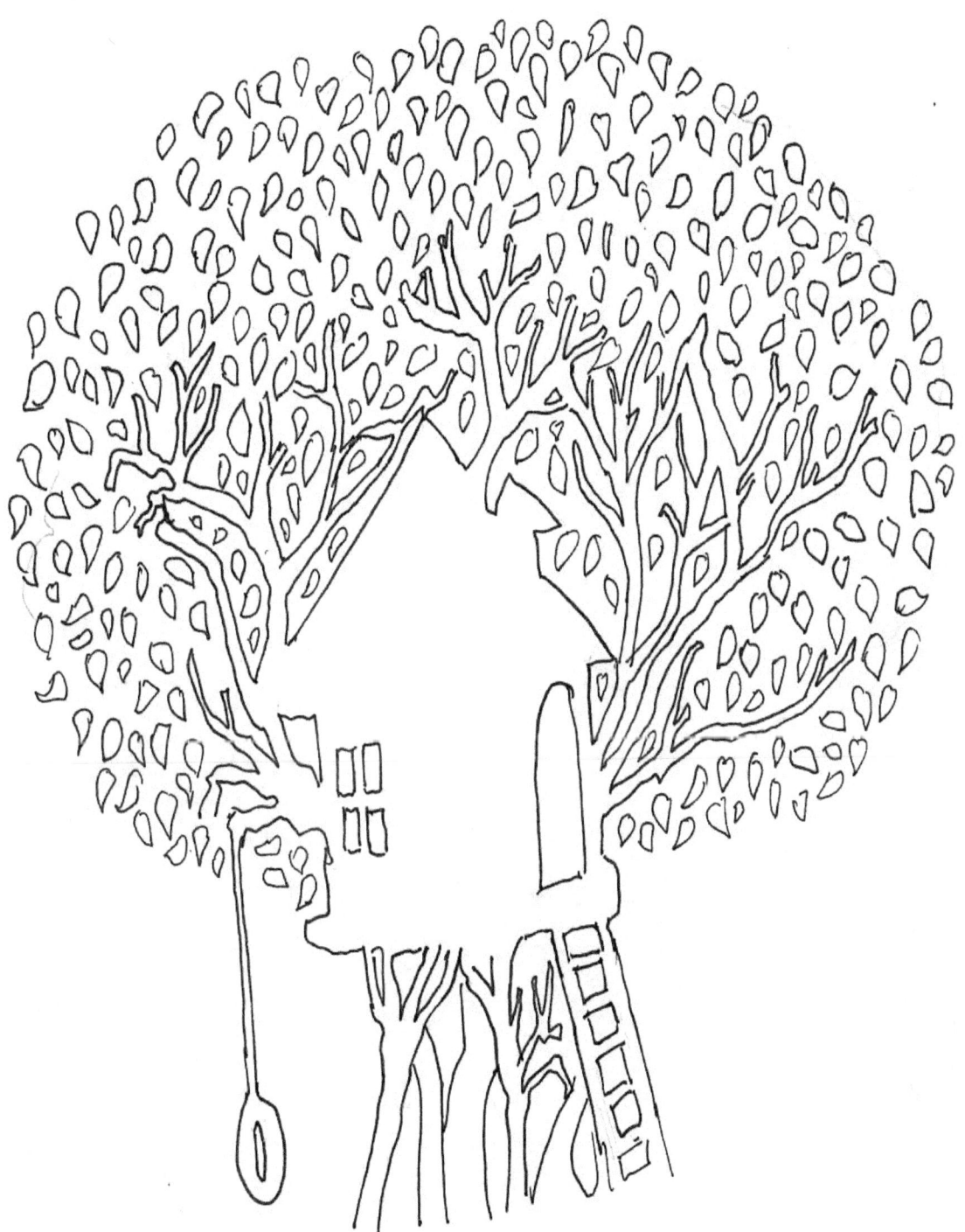

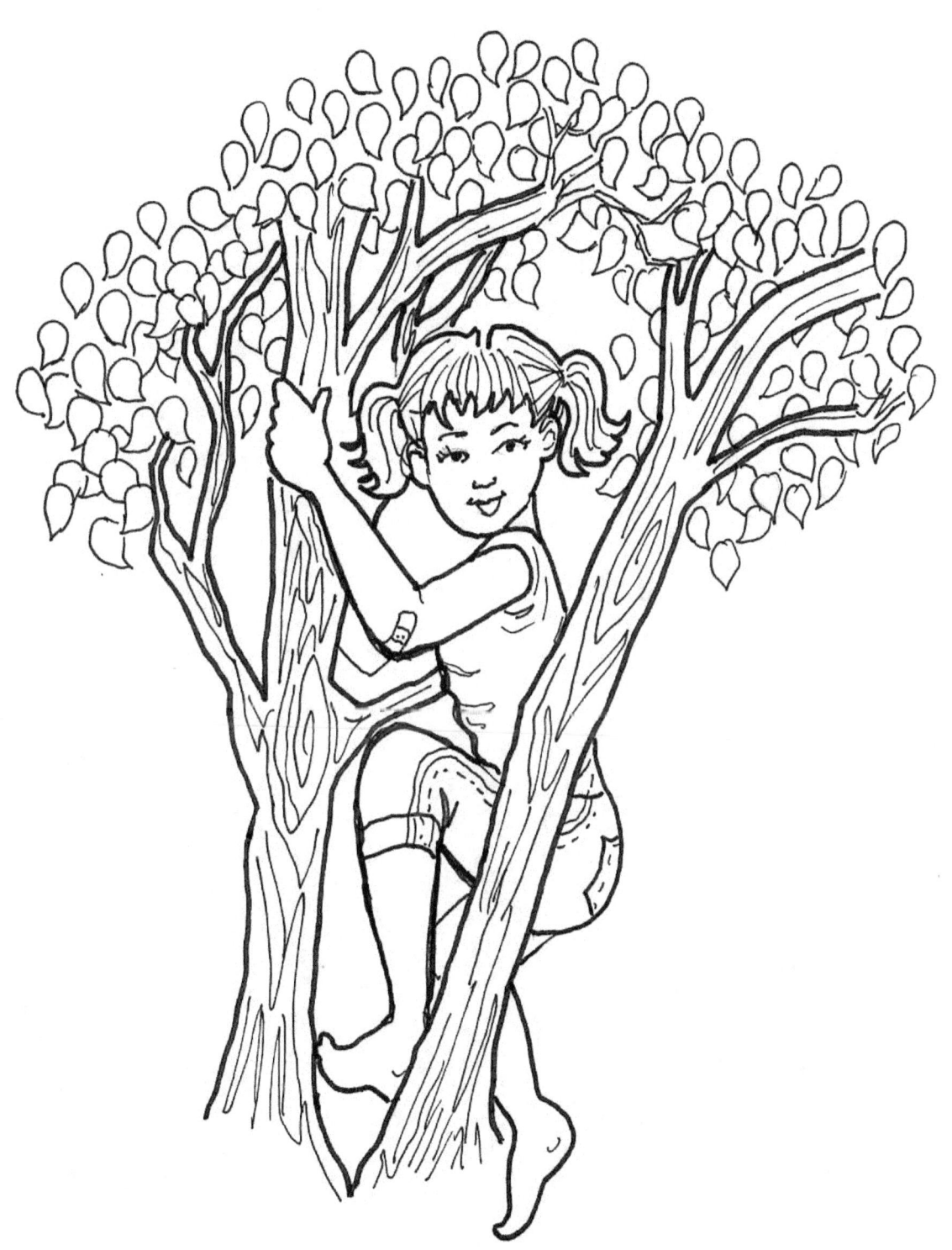

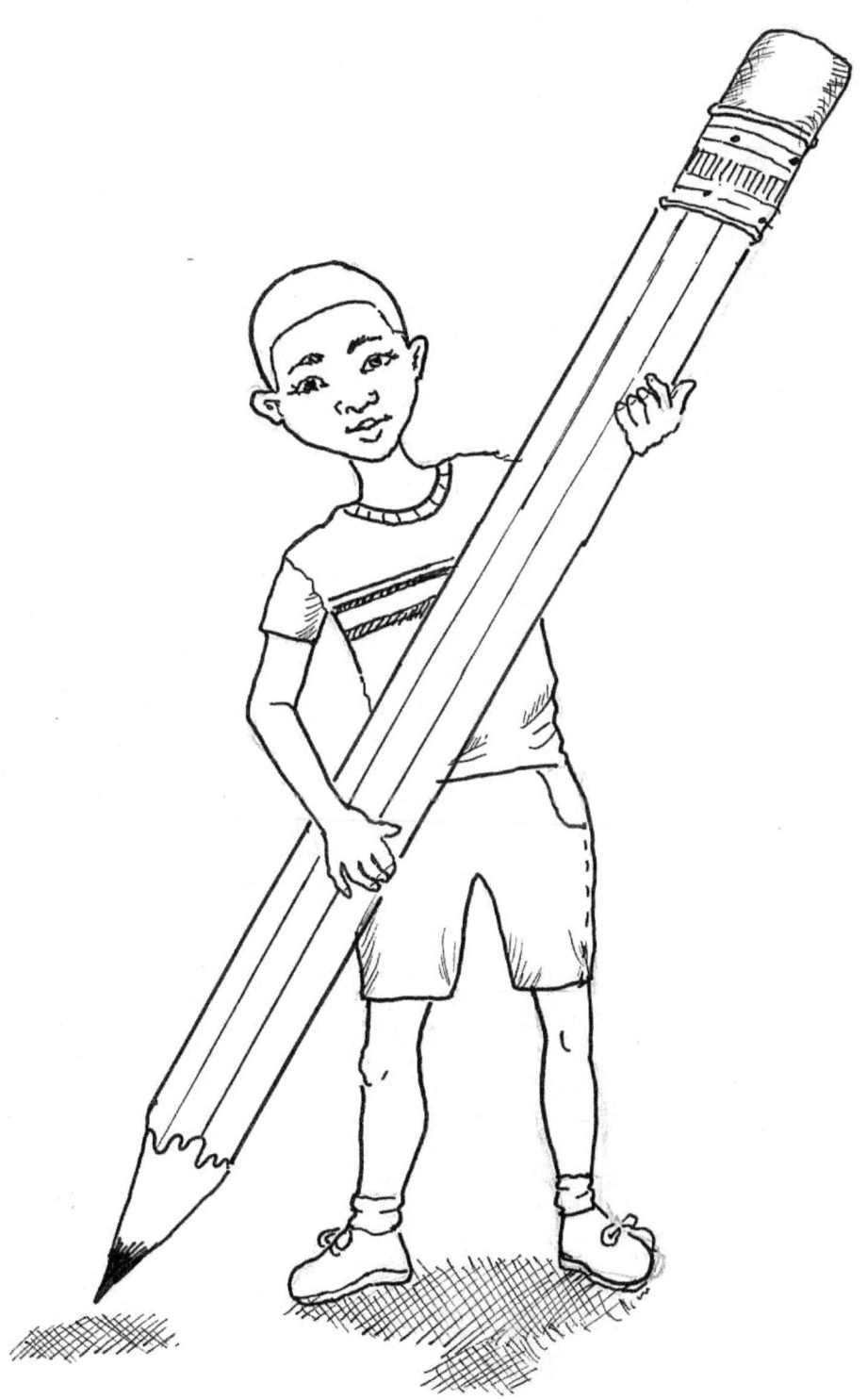

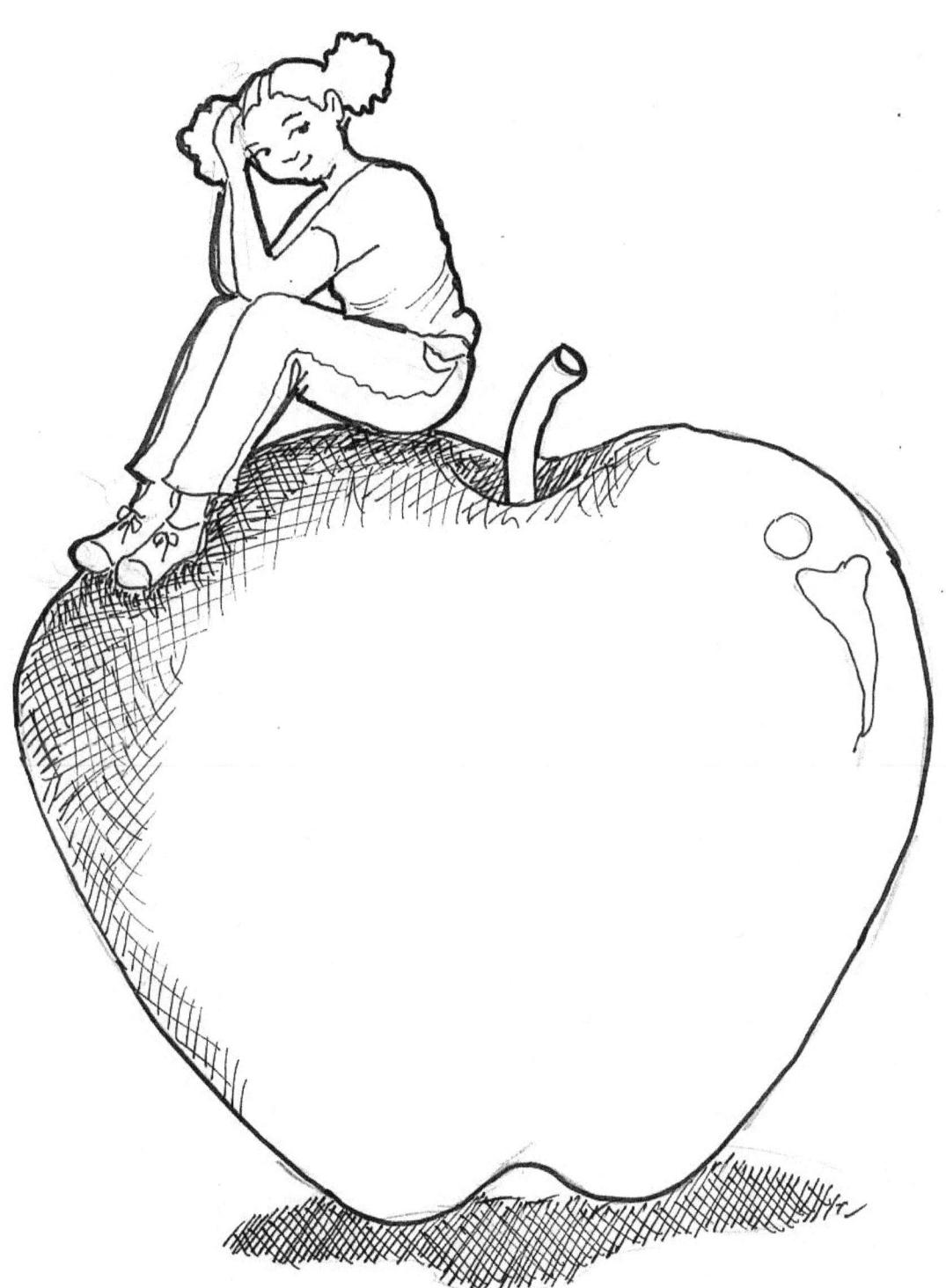

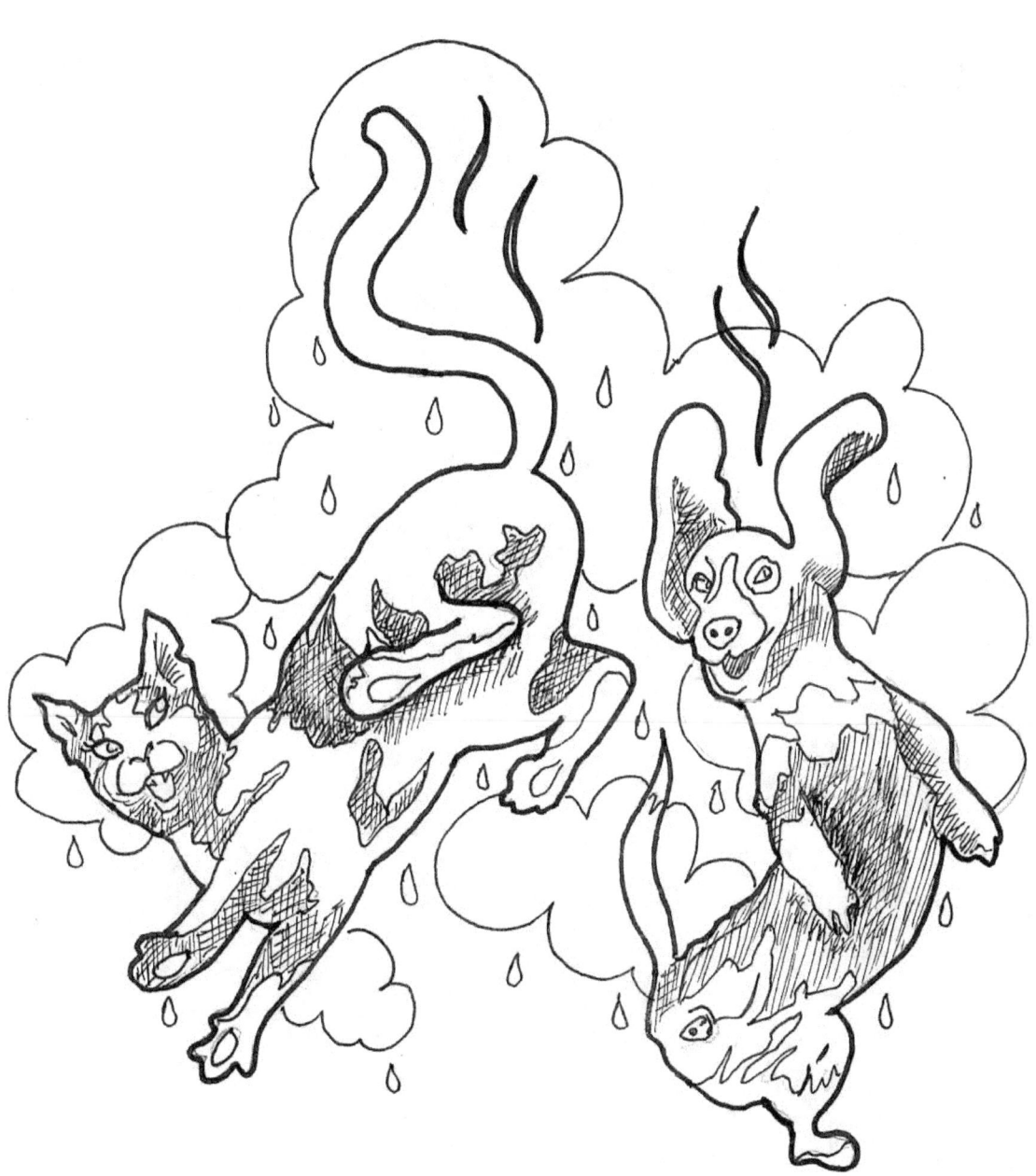

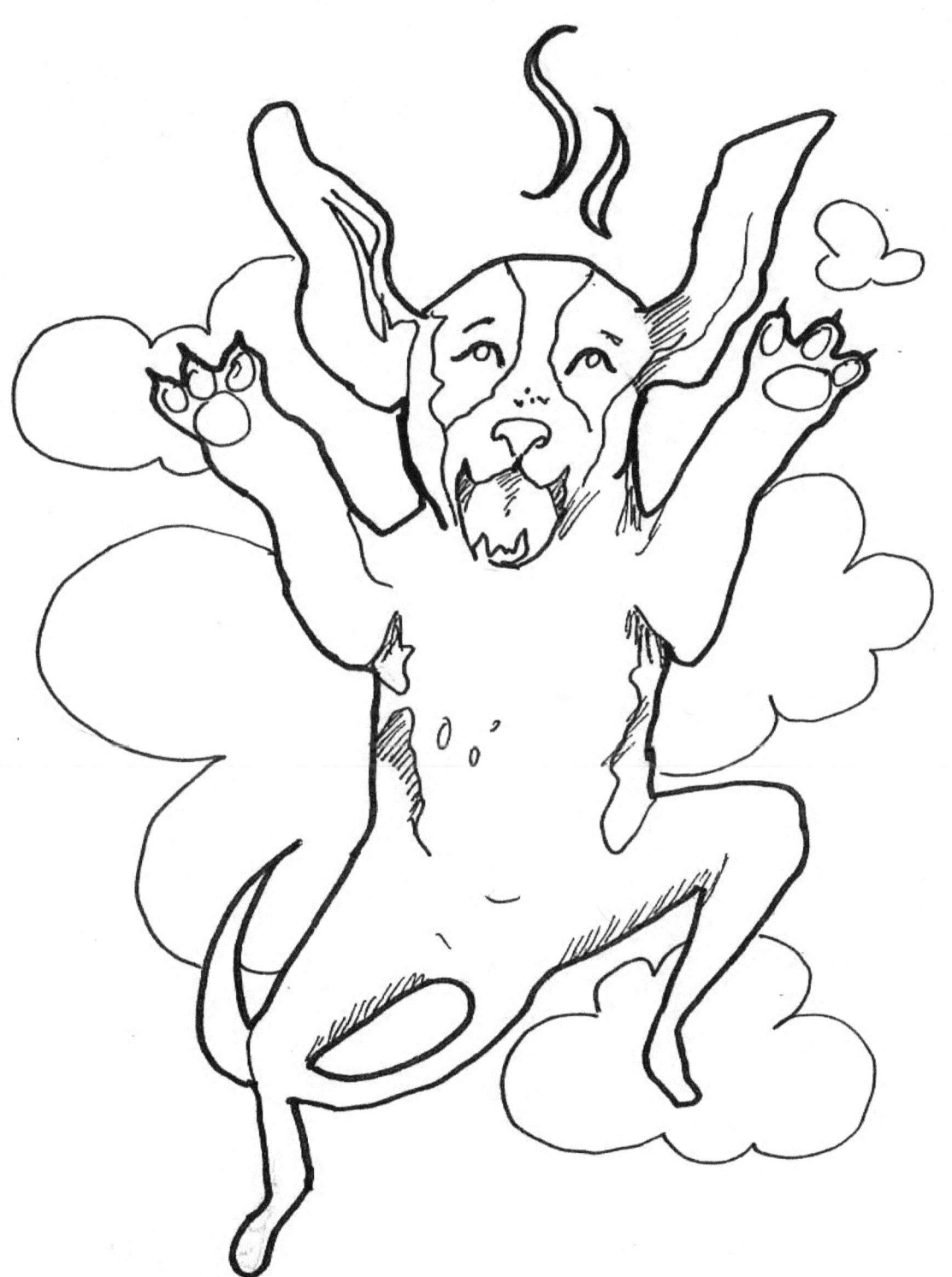

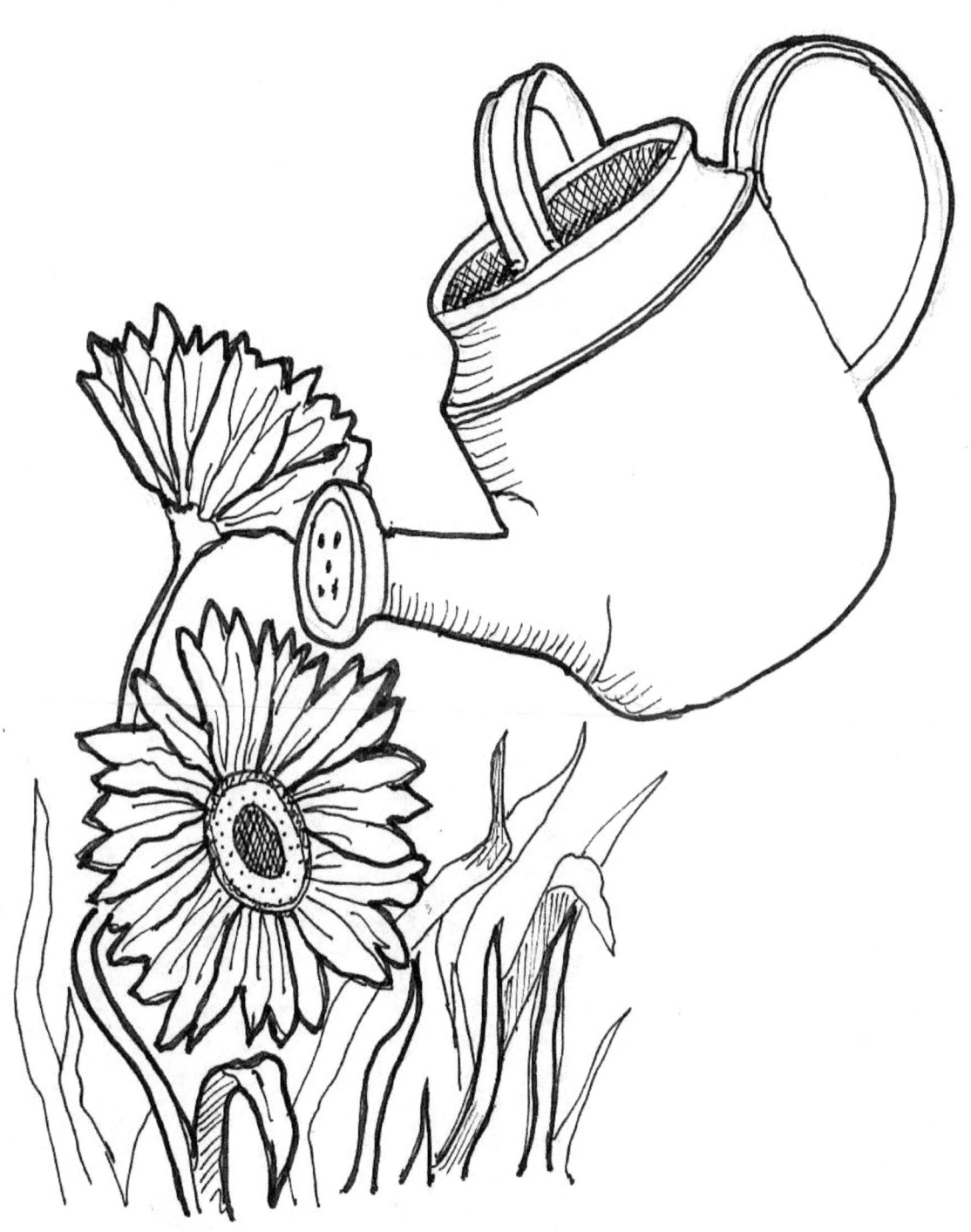

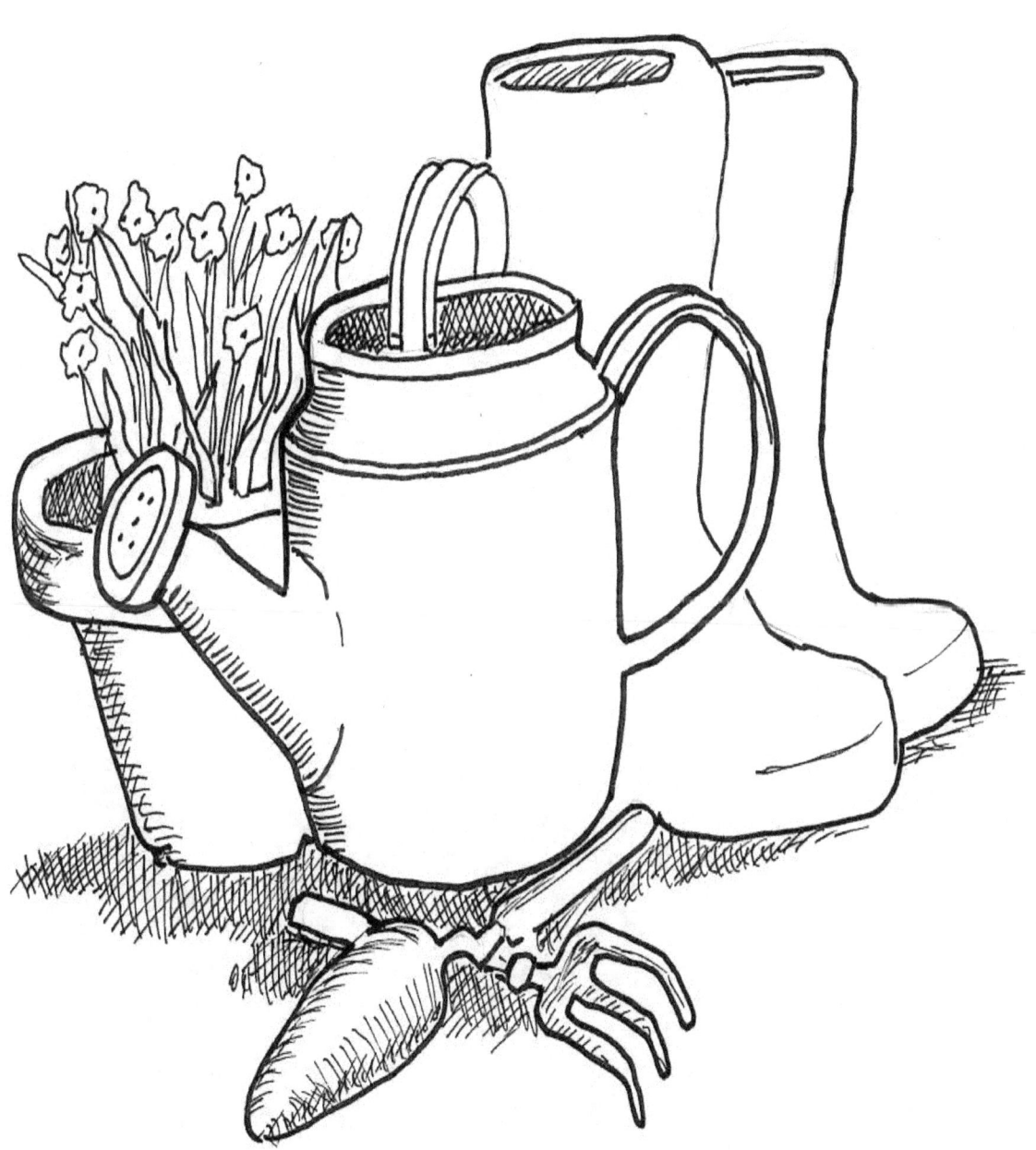

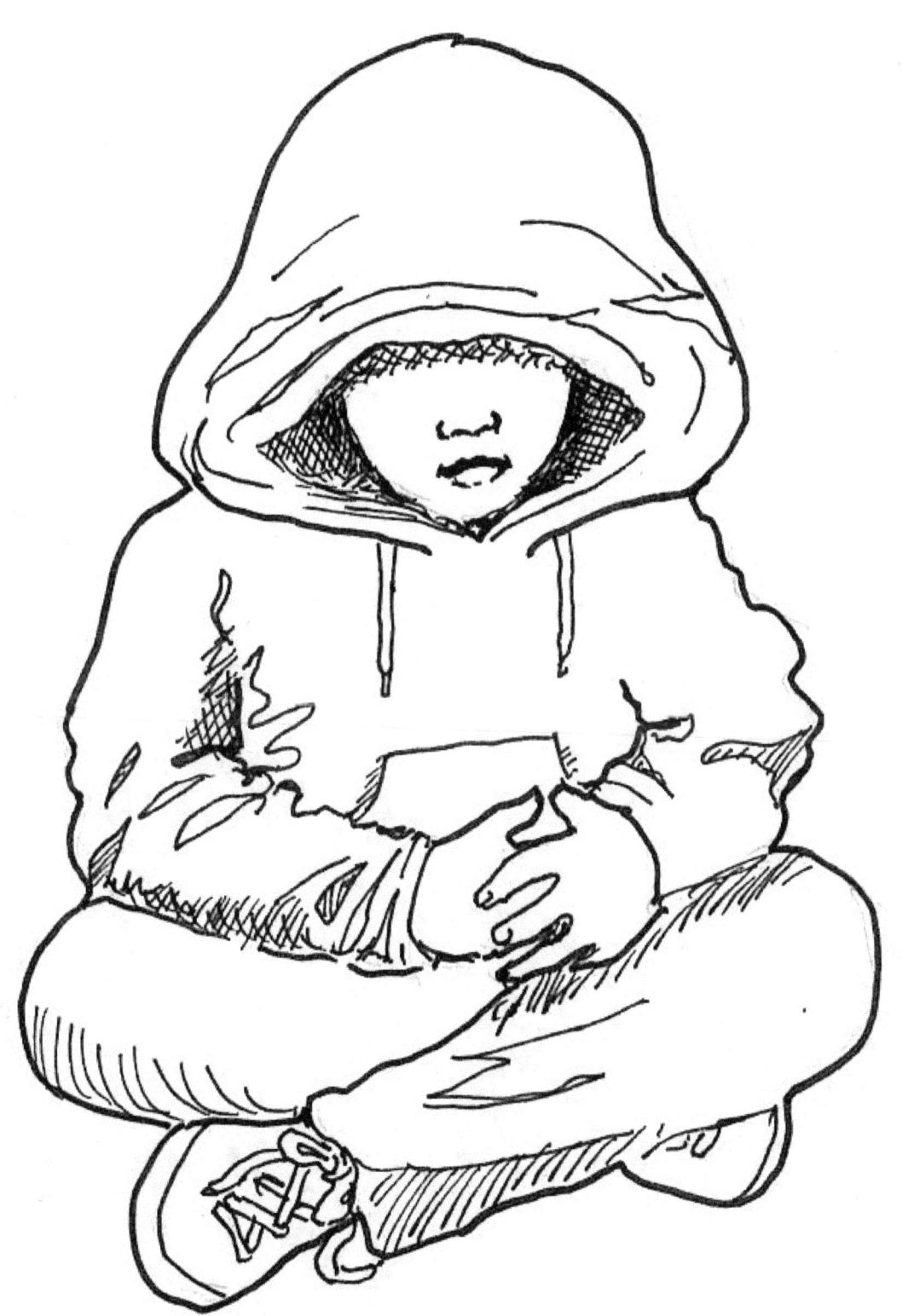

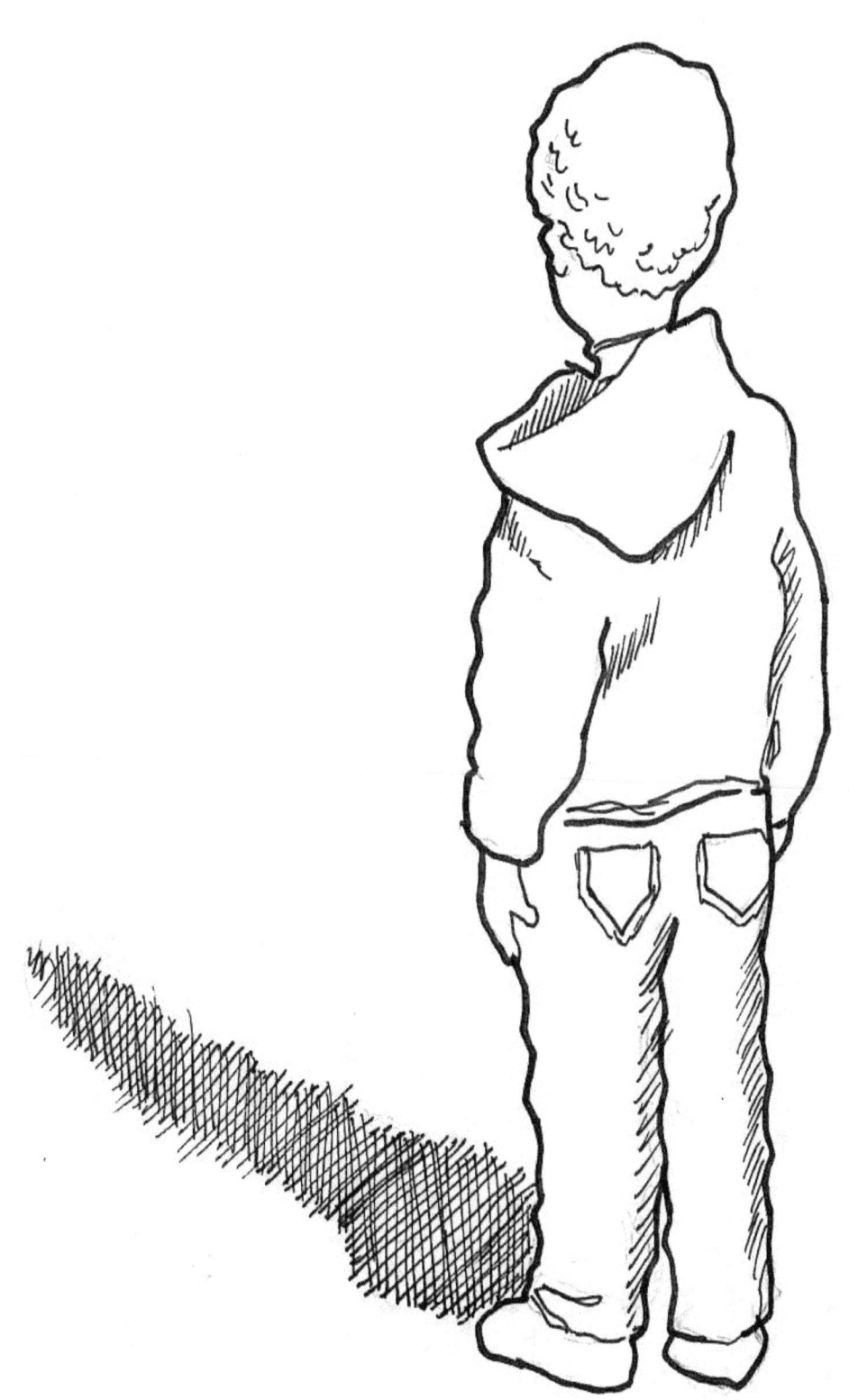

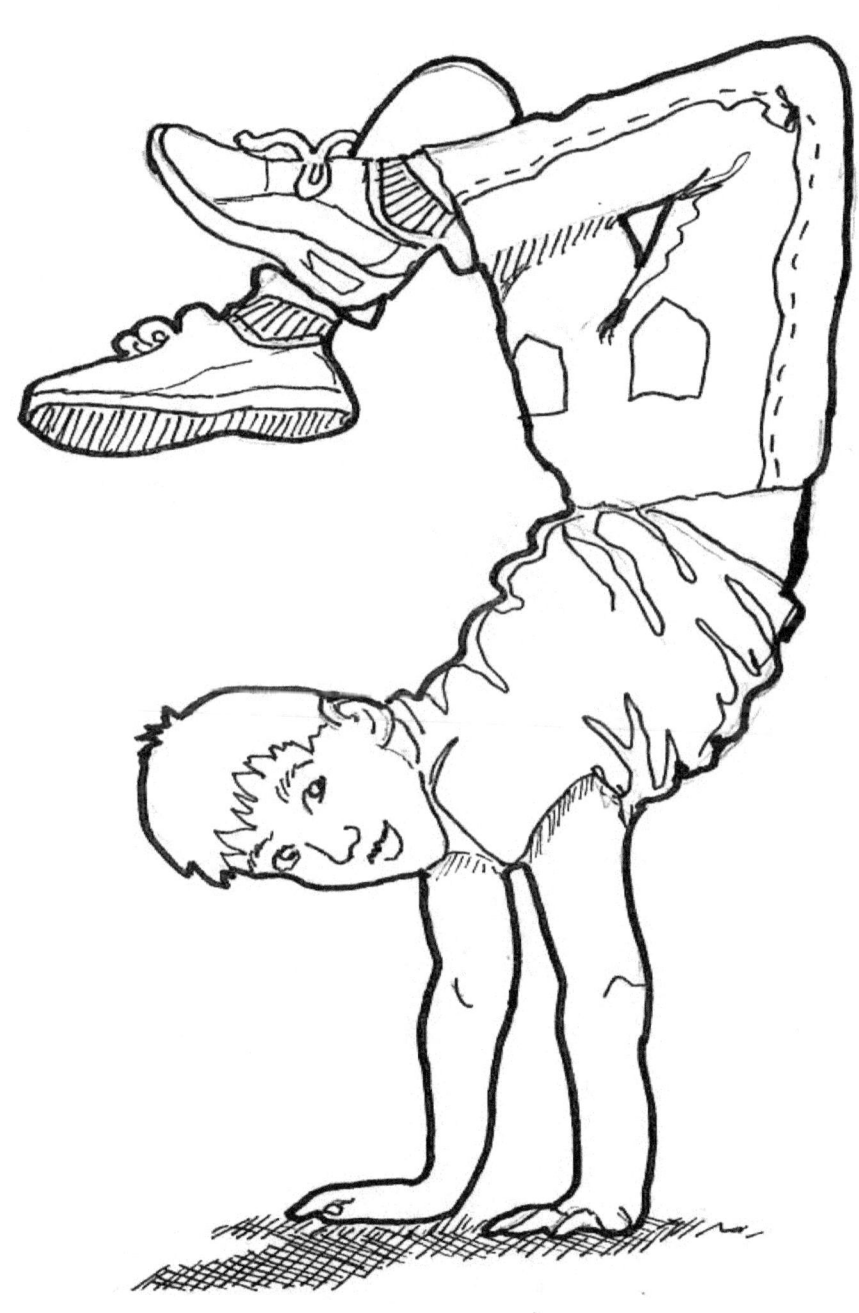

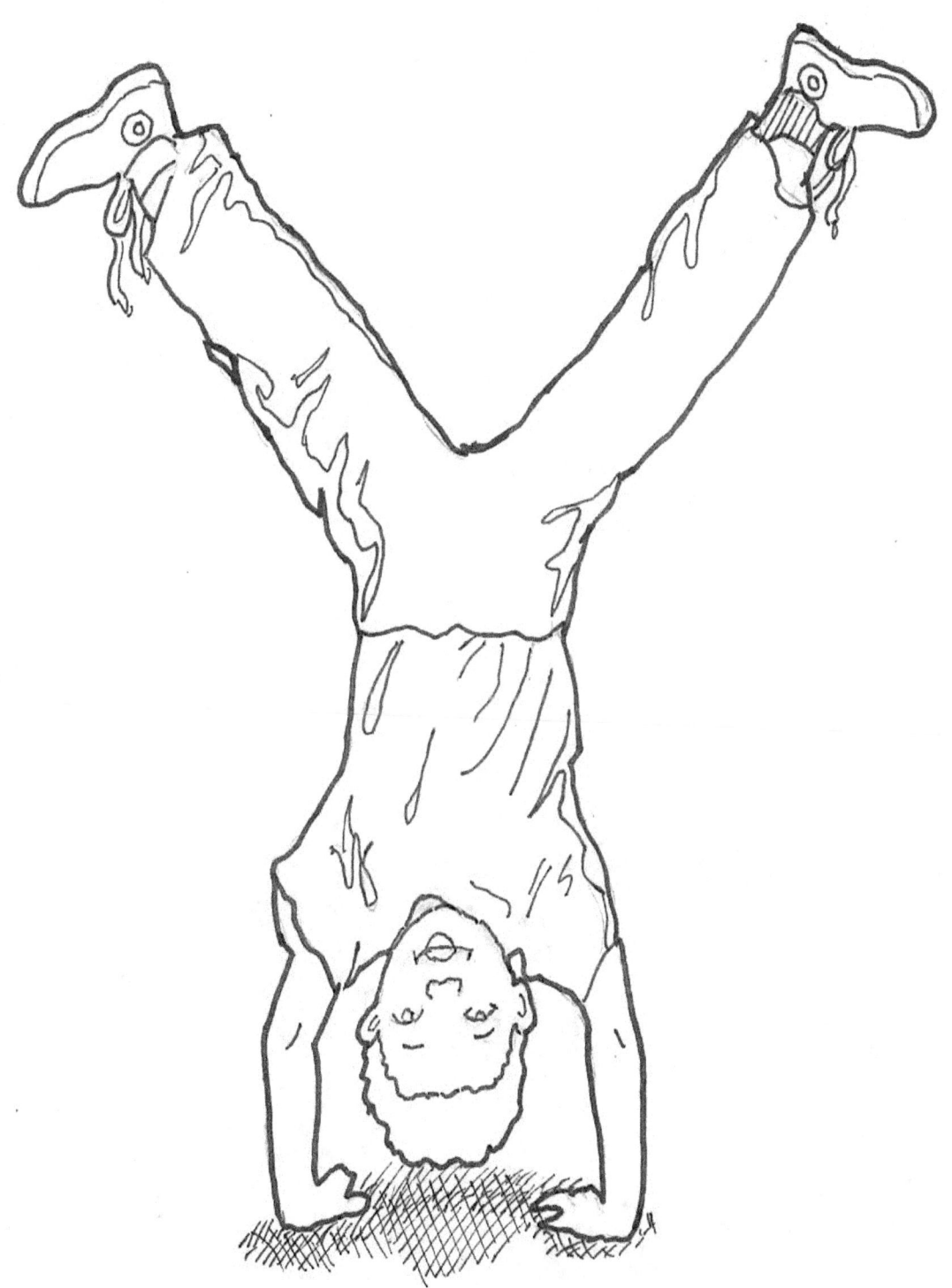

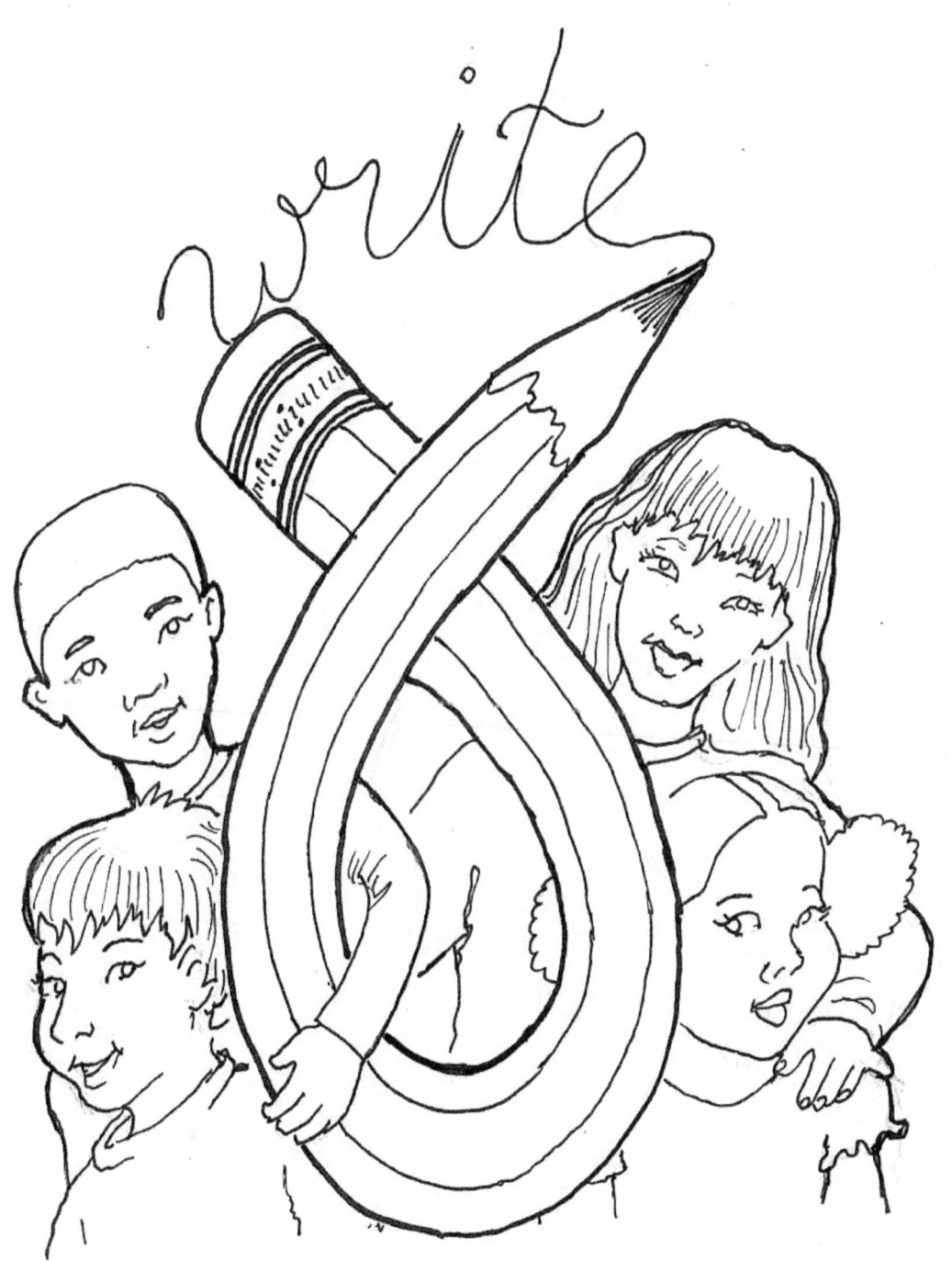

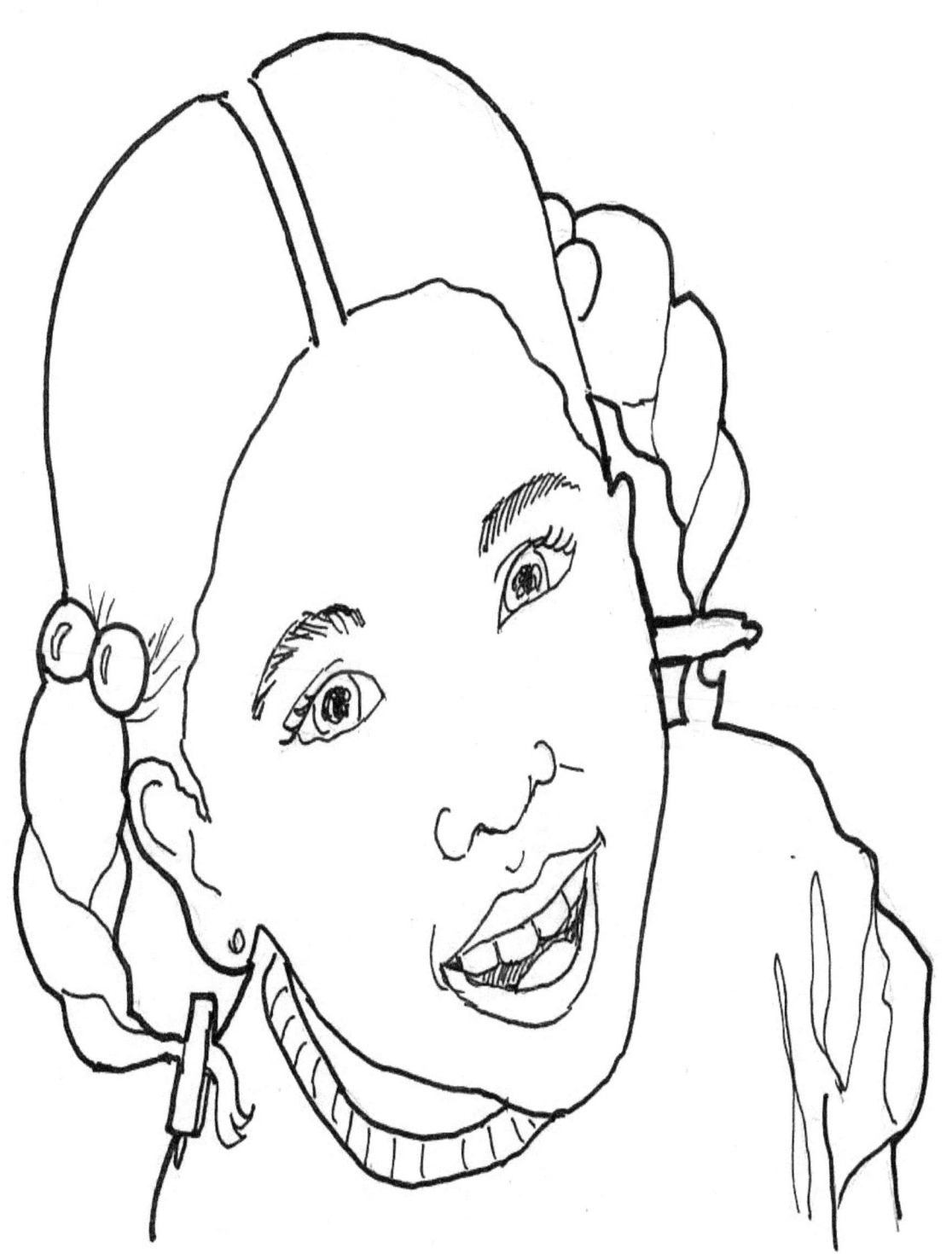

About the Author

Beatrice M. Young is an American writer, living in Eden, North Carolina, with her husband and their cat, Malcolm. She began writing when she was six years old, creating fiction, plays and poems, and journaling. Beatrice loves the writing process so much, she created books she hopes will inspire children to experience the joys of creative writing as much as she does.

The first book in the series is called Scribble Scrabble Writing Journal for Kids. You can purchase additional print copies of Scribble Scrabble Writing Journal books at Etoshapublications, Amazon, Barnes & Noble, and other online retailers. To purchase digital copies visit www.etoshapublications.com. For bulk orders, email beatrice@etoshapublications.com or call 336-280-8321.

If you want to get an automatic email when Beatrice's next book is released, sign up at www.etoshapublications.com. You will only be contacted when a new book is released, your address will never be shared, and you can unsubscribe at anytime.

Word-of-mouth is crucial for any author to succeed. If you enjoyed the book, please consider leaving a review at Amazon. Even if it's only a line or two, it would be a huge help.

Say Hello! You can follow Beatrice on Twitter @etoshapub, get in touch on Facebook.at www.facebook.com/pages/Scribble-Scrabble-Writing-Journal-for-Kids/219086361477544, send an email to beatrice@etoshapublications.com.

www.ingramcontent.com/pod-product-compliance
Lightning Source LLC
Chambersburg PA
CBHW080914170526
45158CB00008B/2106